Biblical Studies from the Catholic Biblical Association of America

GENERAL EDITOR

FRANK J. MATERA

EDITORIAL BOARD

J. E. AGUILAR CHIU • J. ATKINSON
R. BAUTCH • A. HARKINS • P. SPITALER

Previous Volumes in Biblical Studies from the CBA

1.

A Concise Theology of the New Testament
Frank J. Matera

2.

Letters to the Johannine Circle: 1–3 John
Francis J. Moloney, SDB

3.

The Landscape of the Gospels: A Deeper Meaning
Donald Senior, CP

4.

Scripture and Tradition in the Letters of Paul
Ronald D. Witherup, PSS

CHRIST IN THE BOOK OF REVELATION

IAN BOXALL

Biblical Studies
from the Catholic Biblical
Association

No. 5

Paulist Press
New York / Mahwah, NJ

Cover image by sakkmesterke / Shutterstock.com
Cover design by Dawn Massa, Lightly Salted Graphics
Book design by Lynn Else

Library of Congress Cataloging-in-Publication Data
Names: Boxall, Ian, author.
Title: Christ in the Book of Revelation / Ian Boxall.
Description: New York, Mahwah, NJ : Paulist Press, 2021. | Series: Biblical studies from the Catholic biblical association of America ; no. 5 | Includes bibliographical references. | Summary: "The book introduces readers to the multiple dimensions of Christ as portrayed in the Apocalypse" — Provided by publisher.
Identifiers: LCCN 2020053369 (print) | LCCN 2020053370 (ebook) | ISBN 9780809154555 (paperback) | ISBN 9781587688478 (ebook)
Subjects: LCSH: Bible. Revelation — Criticism, interpretation, etc. | Jesus Christ — Biblical teaching. | Second Advent — Biblical teaching.
Classification: LCC BS2825.52 .B695 2021 (print) | LCC BS2825.52 (ebook) DDC 232 — dc23
LC record available at https://lccn.loc.gov/2020053369
LC ebook record available at https://lccn.loc.gov/2020053370

ISBN 978-0-8091-5455-5 (paperback)
ISBN 978-1-58768-847-8 (e-book)

Published by Paulist Press
997 Macarthur Boulevard
Mahwah, New Jersey 07430
www.paulistpress.com

Printed and bound in the
United States of America

In gratitude to Christopher Rowland who first nurtured my
love for the Book of Revelation

Contents

About the Series ix

Preface...xi

Introduction: Christ of the Apocalypse....................................1

Chapter One: The Story of the Apocalypse.........................14

Chapter Two: Titles of Christ in Revelation 31

Chapter Three: The Exalted Son of Man..............................46

Chapter Four: The Victorious Lamb.....................................60

Chapter Five: The Peaceable Warrior...................................74

Chapter Six: The Worship of Christ in Revelation 90

Conclusion: The Christ of the Apocalypse in the
   Life of the Church 105

Select Bibliography 111

About the Series

This series, Biblical Studies from the Catholic Biblical Association of America, seeks to bridge the gap between the technical exegetical work of the academic community and the educational and pastoral needs of the ecclesial community. Combining careful exegesis with a theological understanding of the text, the members of the Catholic Biblical Association of America have written these volumes in a style that is accessible to an educated, nonspecialized audience, without compromising academic integrity.

These volumes deal with biblical texts and themes that are important and vital for the life and ministry of the Church. While some focus on specific biblical books or particular texts, others are concerned with important theological themes, still others with archaeological and geographical issues, and still others with questions of interpretation. Through this series, the members of the Catholic Biblical Association of America are eager to present the results of their research in a way that is relevant to an interested audience that goes beyond the confines of the academic community.

Preface

Like many Catholics of my era, the Book of Revelation, also referred to as the Apocalypse of John, was something of a closed book to me as I was growing up. I heard the occasional reading from Revelation at Mass, such as on the Feast of the Assumption of Our Lady. But for the most part, it remained a puzzle and a mystery. All that changed when I was a graduate student in New Testament at the University of Oxford.

Under the expert guidance of Professor Christopher Rowland, I was introduced to the Apocalypse as a robust articulation of the Gospel of Jesus Christ, one of the richest fruits of the apocalyptic movement that was early Christianity, as well as a potent prophetic critique of injustice and abuse of power in every age. Chris's own engagement with Latin American liberation theology, together with his profound knowledge of Jewish and Christian apocalypses, and his developing interest in Revelation's reception across the centuries, had a profound impact on my own understanding of this extraordinary book.

Elements of that engagement are evident throughout this short volume, which I dedicate to Chris in gratitude for opening up the Apocalypse to me as a graduate student, and for his many years of wisdom, encouragement, and friendship. My hope is this book will assist nonspecialist readers who wish to have a deeper understanding of the Book of Revelation, but have hitherto struggled to find a way in. My purpose is fourfold: (1) to provide a nontechnical introduction to the genre and historical circumstances of the Apocalypse's composition; (2) to provide an overview of the story Revelation tells and the characters it describes; (3) to examine the very different guises under which Christ appears in the Apocalypse, and what these reveal about who Christ is and what he has done; (4) to make connections between the biblical text and how it is encountered by ordinary Christians, particularly in liturgy and in visual art.

I am grateful for the invitation from Frank Matera, Joseph Atkinson, and Enrique Aguilar to contribute to this series, and especially to Frank and Enrique for their careful reading of this manuscript and their helpful suggestions and insights, which have made this a better volume than it might otherwise have been.

Ian Boxall
The Catholic University of America

Introduction

Christ of the Apocalypse

For many Christians, the Book of Revelation (also called the Apocalypse) remains a closed book. Revelation presents a strange, chaotic world of angels and demons, a terrifying dragon and other monsters, and women who turn into cities. It appears to be an outlier among the books of the NT. Yet it also provides one of the richest resources for reflection on the person and work of Christ (Christology). Christ the Lamb, Christ the Root of David, Christ the Alpha and the Omega, Christ the Morning Star: all these familiar titles of Jesus appear in the book.

The Lamb is perhaps the most famous title of all, which helps explain why Revelation has functioned for centuries as the Church's Easter book par excellence. It presents the victory of Christ the Paschal Lamb over sin and death. Even today, the Roman Sunday Lectionary contains readings from the Apocalypse during the Easter Season in Year C. Though this provision covers only a tiny percentage of this extraordinary book (Rev 1:9–11a, 12–13, 17–19; 5:11–14; 7:9, 14b–17; 21:1–5a, 10–14, 22–23; 22:12–14, 16–17, 20), it allows a glimpse into Revelation's vivid, imaginative, and highly symbolic depiction of Jesus.

These lectionary "glimpses" are not the only exposure Catholic Christians have to the Apocalypse. In less obvious ways, the Christ of the Apocalypse is all around us. The great European cathedrals are vivid visual commentaries

1

on the Book of Revelation, and the Jesus it proclaims. The image of Christ as judge is frequently found over cathedral entrances, reminding the entering worshipers of their own final judgment. This image is profoundly indebted to Revelation: Christ enthroned, surrounded by the four living creatures (Rev 4, interpreted as symbols of the four evangelists), a double-edged sword emerging from his mouth (Rev 1:16; 2:12, 16; 19:15, 21). In Chartres Cathedral and La Sainte Chapelle in Paris, magnificent rose windows depict scenes from the Apocalypse, with Christ at the center. A fine set of ceiling bosses in the cloister of Norwich Cathedral in eastern England is another vivid visual interpretation of Revelation's story.

In the case of Europe's Gothic cathedrals, the whole structure functioned as a representation, in stone and glass, of the New Jerusalem, where God and the Lamb make their home (Rev 21–22). The soaring Gothic arches raise the worshiper's view to heaven, from which the celestial city descends, while the richly colored stained glass recalls the twelve precious stones decorating the city's foundations (Rev 21:19–20). Closer to home for inhabitants of the United States, Christ as the Lamb (Rev 5:6) looks down over the main altar in the Basilica of the National Shrine of the Immaculate Conception in Washington, D.C. The Jesus of the Apocalypse is more familiar than might at first appear.

GETTING TO KNOW THE APOCALYPSE

The same familiarity does not extend to the book in which he appears. Many Christians find the Apocalypse obscure, puzzling, or even terrifying. Practically speaking, it is less a book of *revelation*, and more a book of *obfuscation*.

One aim of this short book is to make Revelation a little less obscure. This will assist its primary purpose: to explore Revelation's portrait of Jesus Christ. In doing so, it will make three presumptions. First, it will presume that Revelation was originally intended for specific first-century audiences. Attention to this original context is crucial for appreciating its vision of Christ. This includes its distinctive literary genre, the social location of its first recipients, and the first-century background to its christological titles and images.

Second, this book will presuppose that the Apocalypse conveys its message through telling a story, in which Jesus Christ is a key character. Sensitivity to the unfolding plot will shed light on its Christology. Third, this book will read the Apocalypse, not simply as an early Christian writing, but as the word of God. Revelation has continued to speak to Christians across the centuries, in different circumstances and cultural contexts from its original audiences. We have noted already the popularity of Revelation's Jesus in visual art. We might say that the Apocalypse vividly proclaims, in words and images, the Christian conviction that "Christ has died; Christ is risen; Christ will come again."

These three foundational presuppositions require complementary scholarly methods: historical-critical (to understand Revelation in its original, first-century context), narrative-critical (to appreciate how the text works as story), and reception-historical (to learn from those who have read, heard, or visualized the Apocalypse in the intervening centuries).

WHAT KIND OF BOOK?

The opening of a text is revealing. It not only provokes interest, encouraging readers to continue reading. It also conveys important information about its genre, and its intended readership or audience. Both are of interest to historical critics. Historical criticism acknowledges that Revelation was written at a specific time in history, addressing specific audiences inhabiting cultural contexts different from our own. It therefore pays close attention to the book's genre and modes of expression, and how these would have been understood at the time of its composition. It considers what the text reveals about the author's purpose, and about its original recipients.

Revelation's opening chapter indicates that it is a book of mixed genre. It presents itself as a book of prophecy (Rev 1:3), opens like a circular letter (1:4–5), and contains elements of other types of literature, including a fragment of liturgy (1:5b–6), a prophetic oracle (1:7), and a beatitude (1:3). But Revelation also exhibits a family resemblance to Jewish and early Christian books (e.g., Daniel; 1 Enoch; 4 Ezra; Apocalypse of Paul) known as apocalypses. Indeed, Revelation's opening word *apokalypsis* ("revelation" or "unveiling") has given this genre its name.

As a "prophetic message" (Rev 1:3), Revelation conveys the word of the Lord, of both comfort and challenge, to his people. John, by implication, is the mediating prophet. The letter opening at verses 4–5a, resembling other early Christian letters, identifies the intended recipients of this written prophecy: "the seven churches in Asia."

OPENINGS OF NT LETTERS

"Paul, Silvanus, and Timothy to the church of the
Thessalonians in God the Father and the Lord Jesus
Christ: grace to you and peace" (1 Thess 1:1).
"Paul, an apostle of Christ Jesus by the will of God, and
Timothy our brother, to the church of God that is in

Corinth, with all the holy ones throughout Achaia: grace to you and peace from God our Father and the Lord Jesus Christ" (2 Cor 1:1–2).

"Symeon Peter, a slave and apostle of Jesus Christ, to those who have received a faith of equal value to ours through the righteousness of our God and savior Jesus Christ: may grace and peace be yours in abundance through knowledge of God and of Jesus our Lord" (2 Pet 1:1–2).

"John, to the seven churches in Asia: grace to you and peace from him who is and who was and who is to come, and from the seven spirits before his throne, and from Jesus Christ, the faithful witness, the firstborn of the dead and ruler of the kings of the earth" (Rev 1:4–5a).

Most modern readers are struck by Revelation's strange, apocalyptic features. Apocalypses are narrative works in which heavenly secrets are unveiled to a privileged human visionary by a heavenly intermediary such as an angel. These secrets often concern history, or the events of the end (eschatology), offering hope and reassurance to the readers of God's plan for them. However, they may also relate to cosmology, astronomy, or the origins of evil. The worldview of apocalypses is dualistic, distinguishing sharply between heaven and earth, and between the righteous and unrighteous. Moreover, the revelation is frequently conveyed through symbolic, often surreal visions. The Italian academic Umberto Eco (1932–2016), author of the famous novel *The Name of the Rose*, famously defined *apocalypse* as "the vision of the outsider, or of the artist who makes us see by making things strange."[1]

Revelation contains several features typical of an apocalypse. It describes the revelation of heavenly secrets to a human recipient, John of Patmos (Rev 1:1, 9–20). It contains a dualistic worldview, with a sharp (though temporary) contrast between heaven and earth, and a division of characters according to their allegiance to God or to the devil/dragon (though it is possible to "repent" and move from the unrighteous to the righteous category, e.g., Rev 2:5, 16, 21; 3:3, 19; 9:21; 16:9). Its symbolic visions present human actors in animal form (e.g., 5:6–14), including monsters symbolizing political tyrants or the empires they rule (13:1–10; 17:3, 7–8).

The book also uses symbolic numbers. Most prominent is seven (e.g., seven seals, seven trumpets, seven bowls), symbolizing perfection, the sum of three (a number associated with the deity, e.g., 1:4, 8; 4:8) and four (the number of the created world, e.g., 4:6, 8; 7:1). Other important numbers include twelve (three multiplied by four), signifying the twelve tribes of Israel; six, one less than seven and therefore symbolizing imperfection (as in 666, the number of the beast, 13:18); and three and a half (half of seven), denoting a limited period of persecution for God's people. The latter number occurs in different forms, each denoting three-and-a-half years: "a time, times, and half a time" (Rev 12:14, author's translation; see Dan 7:25; 12:7), "forty-two months" (Rev 11:2; 13:5), and "twelve hundred and sixty days" (11:3; 12:6).

Revelation's apocalyptic features demonstrate Eco's observation about making us see "by making things strange." For example, John describes how he turned to *see* the voice that was speaking with him (1:12). Voices are normally heard, not seen! John is told of a great multitude who

---

1. Umberto Eco, *Apocalypse Postponed*, ed. Robert Lumley (Bloomington: Indiana University Press, 1994), 3.

have washed their robes and made them white in the blood of the Lamb (7:14). This is counterintuitive, since blood ordinarily makes clothing red. Such language stretches the imagination almost to breaking point. The Apocalypse forces us to see the world differently, and to reassess our perception of reality accordingly.

FEATURES OF APOCALYPSES

- ◆ Narrative framework
- ◆ Revelation of heavenly mysteries by a heavenly mediator
- ◆ Dualistic worldview
- ◆ Symbolic visions
- ◆ Numerical symbolism

THE APOCALYPSE'S FIRST AUDIENCES

Revelation 1 also provides important information about the book's intended recipients. It is more accurate to call these original recipients "audiences" than "readers," given Revelation 1:3: "Blessed is the one who reads aloud and blessed are those who listen to this prophetic message and heed what is written in it, for the appointed time is near." This beatitude presupposes low levels of literacy in the ancient world. We should envisage the Apocalypse being read aloud by one individual (a reader or lector) to the assembled congregation. Thus, the earliest reception of Revelation would have been an aural experience. This helps explain the repeated refrain: "Whoever has ears ought to hear what the Spirit says to the churches" (2:7, 11, 17, 29; 3:6, 13, 22).

The original audiences are "the seven churches in Asia" (1:4). "Asia" refers to the Roman province of that name, situated on the western edge of Asia Minor (modern western Turkey). Verse 11 identifies the cities where these congregations were located: "Ephesus, Smyrna, Pergamum, Thyatira, Sardis, Philadelphia, and Laodicea." Some of these were major cities by ancient standards (Ephesus and Pergamum, e.g., had estimated populations of around 200,000 and 120,000, respectively). Thyatira, by contrast, was much smaller and more provincial. These seven were not the only Asian cities with churches in the late first century CE. Both Colossae and Hierapolis were part of the Pauline mission (Col 1:2; 4:13), while the churches at Tralles and Magnesia-on-the-Meander were well established by the time of Ignatius of Antioch in the early second century. That John only mentions seven congregations is probably because seven symbolizes perfection: they stand for the whole church.

John addresses these "seven churches" from the small island of Patmos (Rev 1:9), located in the Aegean Sea approximately sixty miles southwest of Ephesus. Scholars are divided over the identity of this "John," and the reason for his presence on Patmos. Early tradition identifies him as John "one of the apostles of Christ" (Justin Martyr, *Trypho* 81), assumed to be the son of Zebedee, or alternatively "the elder John" of Ephesus (Eusebius, *H.E.* 3.39.6). The author simply calls himself "John" (Rev 1:4, 9; 22:8), and presents himself as a prophet-visionary. He was on Patmos "on account of the word of God and the testimony of Jesus" (1:9, author's translation). This statement is normally understood to mean that John was exiled to Patmos by Roman authorities due to his preaching, as implied in the NABRE translation: "because I proclaimed God's word and gave testimony to Jesus." Alternatively, it could mean that he was directed to Patmos as a place to receive visions, or that he went to the island as part of his missionary activity.

The date of writing is also a matter of scholarly discussion. The majority view, based on the late second-century testimony of Irenaeus (*Adv. Haer.* 5.30.3), is that John wrote toward the end of Domitian's reign (81–96). An alternative view would date Revelation almost three decades earlier, in the turbulent years after the death of Nero in 68 CE, whether during the short-lived reign of Galba (68–69) or early in the reign of Vespasian (69–79).

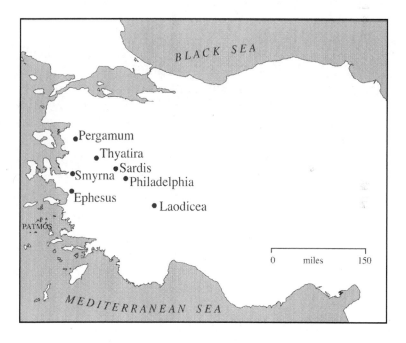

Map: Patmos and the Seven Churches

There is more clarity about the social situation of the seven churches. The Christ of the Apocalypse addresses them directly, through their respective "angel," in the seven messages of Revelation 2 – 3. Although Revelation has often been read as a book written to console persecuted Christians, the seven messages reveal a more complex picture. Only one actual martyr is mentioned by name, Antipas of Pergamum (2:13), and his death is an event of the past. Of the seven churches, only two receive undiluted praise (those in Smyrna and Philadelphia, 2:8–11; 3:7–13). The major issue seems to be the appropriate relationship between followers of Jesus and their surrounding Roman culture. This question apparently divided the congregations. Revelation speaks of so-called apostles (2:2), a group called "the Nicolaitans" (2:6, 15), people "who hold to the teaching of Balaam" (2:14; cf. Num 22 – 24), and a rival prophet John names "Jezebel" (Rev 2:20; cf. 1 Kgs 19:1–2). In addition, the messages to Smyrna and Philadelphia hint at tensions between followers of Jesus and other Jews (caustically referred to as "the assembly [or synagogue] of Satan," Rev 2:9; 3:9).

Revelation unveils Roman culture as demonic and advocates a strongly countercultural stance. Rome may appear to be beneficent, and the cities of Asia had profited economically, and enhanced their urban honor, because of Roman expansion. But Rome has a darker, monstrous side, which is only visible by divine revelation (13:1–10; 17:1–18). John's urgent message to many in the seven congregations, therefore, is that they reassess their priorities and ultimate commitments.

THE STORY AND ITS CHARACTERS

It is often difficult for the reader of the Apocalypse to see the forest for the trees. Even when read as an unfolding story, Revelation's repetitions, subplots, and the changing guise of major characters can result in loss of focus. It is crucial, therefore, for readers to step back and appreciate the big picture.

Narrative criticism will be employed to sketch this big picture. Narrative criticism is less interested in historical origins than on a text's inner workings and coherence. Meaning is found through attention to a book's plot, the portrayal of its characters, and the point of view it espouses. Narrative criticism is primarily used in NT studies to understand the Gospels as stories of Jesus. However, it has also proved beneficial for interpreting the Apocalypse, which also tells a story, albeit one closer to modern fantasy literature than a biography or typical novel. Revelation contains a rich cast of characters, both human and nonhuman, angelic and demonic. Many are "supporting actors," who appear once or only occasionally, adding color to the overall narrative or functioning as "foils" to the main characters. A few, however, play a more central role, and their identity unfolds as the story progresses. Chief among these are the figures of God (frequently called "the one seated on the throne"), and Jesus Christ, whose character appears in several different, but complementary guises. On the other side are the dragon and his cronies the beasts, whose point of view is suspect and to be rejected.

Yet Revelation's story is not only shaped by the interactions between its characters. It also evokes older stories. Chief among these is the story of the exodus. Revelation contains multiple echoes of this foundational narrative of the liberation of God's people from Egypt. Even the central image of Christ, the victorious Lamb, is shaped in part by the memory of the Passover lamb (Exod 12). Revelation also alludes to the Eden story (Rev 12), and the return from exile in Babylon (Rev 17–18; 21–22). Some scholars even see

11

the broad sweep of salvation history, from exodus to exile, embedded in the seven messages of Revelation 2–3.[2]

In addition, Greco-Roman mythology, familiar to the inhabitants of Roman Asia, has also left its mark. Revelation 12 recalls the story of the birth of Apollo, whose pregnant mother Leto was threatened by the dragon Python, and reworks it to tell the story of Christ.

THE APOCALYPSE AS SCRIPTURE

Appreciating the social setting of Revelation's original audiences is crucial for understanding the prophetic message of the book. Grasping the big picture of Revelation's story also facilitates understanding. But, as the word of God, the message of the Apocalypse is not confined to first-century Christians living under the shadow of imperial Rome. Its comforting yet challenging message has continued to speak to fresh Christian audiences across the centuries. This is especially the case with its vivid depiction of Jesus as the slaughtered yet victorious Lamb.

Here we venture into the realms of reception history, that is, the history of how the text has been received from the first century to the present day. Reception historians are not simply interested in how biblical scholars and other theological "experts" have interpreted the book. They also examine its effects at the popular level, among ordinary Christians, and its wider cultural impact in music, visual art,

---

2. Most recently, Francis J. Moloney, *The Apocalypse of John: A Commentary* (Grand Rapids: Baker Academic, 2020), 61–86.

literature, drama, and even politics. Aspects of the reception history of Revelation will be interwoven into this book.[3]

Priority will be given to the christological reception: how the Christ of the Apocalypse has been understood. One unfortunate aspect of popular reception has been to prioritize Revelation's "darker side": focus on the devil, or speculation about the identity and number of the beast, or the "antichrist" (ironically, a term that never occurs in the book). A simple Google search for "Book of Revelation" will demonstrate this fascination with evil. Yet its opening words tell a very different story: "The revelation of Jesus Christ" (1:1). Christ is the primary actor in the story. The Apocalypse is not meant primarily to instill fear or panic, but trust in the victory of Christ. This christological focus provides the question this book seeks to answer: Who is the Christ of the Apocalypse?

———————————

Chapter 1 will offer an overview of Revelation's story, to help orient the reader to the big picture. Subsequent chapters will examine the different "portraits" of Jesus within the unfolding narrative of John's visions, consider their meaning against Revelation's Jewish and Greco-Roman background, and explore how these striking images of Christ have continued to speak to Christians in subsequent centuries. The book will conclude with some reflections on how these complementary images deepen our understanding of Christ, and his relationship to his people.

———————————

3. For an excellent study of the reception history of Revelation, see Judith Kovacs and Christopher Rowland, *Revelation: The Apocalypse of Jesus Christ*, Blackwell Bible Commentaries (Malden, MA: Blackwell, 2004).

CHAPTER ONE

The Story of the Apocalypse

Recent scholarship on the Book of Revelation takes seriously its narrative unity.[1] While earlier commentators often concentrated on the book's complexities and awkward transitions (positing the combining of sources, different editions, or even several authors), many now search for an underlying coherence. This holistic way of reading the Apocalypse reminds us of its story character. Revelation recounts the journey of its narrator, "John," from an identifiable place on the earth ("the island called Patmos," Rev 1:9), into the heavenly throne room, where he witnesses a series of visions, some located in heaven, others apparently on earth. Seeing the big picture of this story is crucial for making sense of its details. Narrative criticism, therefore, complements historical criticism's interest in the meaning of Revelation for its original audiences, the seven churches of Asia. A narrative-critical reading invites the reader to enter the visionary world that John describes, accompany John on his journey, and experience the emotions he experiences.

Narrative critics examine features such as setting, point of view, and characterization to understand the text's

---

1. Examples include D. L. Barr, *Tales of the End: A Narrative Commentary on the Book of Revelation* (Santa Rosa, CA: Polebridge Press, 1998); J. L. Resseguie, *The Revelation of John: A Narrative Commentary* (Grand Rapids: Baker Academic, 2009).

plot. Settings may be geographical (e.g., heaven, earth, the abyss, Patmos, Babylon, Armageddon), or temporal (e.g., "on the Lord's day," "for ten days," "for a thousand years"). The text's point of view is the perspective from which it is written, the values it espouses. In Revelation, God and his heavenly agents are the voices to be trusted, while the perspective of the dragon and his minions (e.g., the beast from the sea, the beast from the earth) deceives people, and is to be rejected. John's voice, too, is reliable, as he is the prophetic servant of God and Christ. Canticles sung in praise of God or the Lamb (e.g., 4:11; 5:9–10; 11:17–18) can also be expected to convey Revelation's trustworthy point of view. By contrast, the statement of the beast's supremacy by its worshipers (13:4: "Who can compare with the beast or who can fight against it?") is unreliable.

In the process of telling its story, Revelation introduces a panoply of characters, some fantastic (a seven-headed dragon and beast; a seven-horned, seven-eyed lamb; monstrous hybrid locusts), some less so (angels, twenty-four elders, a pregnant woman). The description of these characters clarifies that the journey John undertakes reveals a cosmos in conflict. Like other apocalypses, Revelation uses dualistic language to divide reality. Many characters can be identified as allied either to God and the Lamb on the one side, or the devil (symbolized by the dragon, 12:3–4; 20:2) and his associates on the other. The earth, however, remains contested territory. Hence, the position of other characters (e.g., those Revelation calls "the inhabitants of the earth") also remains contested. This ambiguity even extends to some members of the seven churches of Asia to whom John writes. From John's perspective, they are associated too closely with the beast or monster from the sea (a symbol of imperial Rome, politically and culturally dominant in the cities where these churches were located).

CHRIST IN THE BOOK OF REVELATION

Narrative criticism's quest for Revelation's structure and plot is less straightforward. There are certainly sections where the structure is clear (e.g., the sequences of seven messages, seven seals, seven trumpets, and seven bowls, 2–3; 6:1–8:1; 8:2–11:18; 15:5–16:21). Elsewhere, however, the structure breaks down, and the reader struggles to makes sense of the intervening material (e.g., 11:19–15:4). Moreover, some sections of the book appear to repeat earlier material (notably the strong echoes of the plagues of Egypt in both chaps. 8–9 and 16). As early as the third century, commentators suggested that the book repeats itself, rather than developing in a linear fashion from beginning to end. It may be helpful here to remember John's claim that visionary experience underlies his book, even if its final form exhibits careful editing and conscious reflection on that experience. If we take this claim to visionary experience seriously, then this might partially explain the chaotic, dream-like quality of certain sections of the book, including swift scene changes and kaleidoscopic images.

In many ways, modern narrative critics are in tune with medieval interpreters of the Apocalypse, especially those who interpreted the book through visual art. Memorable examples of their work include the famous Anglo-Norman apocalypse manuscripts of the thirteenth and fourteenth centuries, like the *Trinity Apocalypse* (Trinity College, Cambridge), or the *Cloisters Apocalypse* (The Cloisters, Metropolitan Museum of Art, New York), in which the story of Revelation unfolds visually page by page. These colorful and richly illustrated manuscripts allow the viewer to participate in John's journey from Patmos to heaven and back again. Closely related to these manuscript images are the famous fourteenth-century Angers Apocalypse tapestries, now housed in a purpose-built gallery in the Château of Angers, France. Visitors can literally "walk through" the story of the Book of Revelation, visually displayed on the gallery's walls.

What follows in the remainder of this chapter is one possible walk through of Revelation's story. This will serve as an orienting overview for readers, in preparation for our examination of the Christ that the Apocalypse reveals.

STRUCTURE OF THE APOCALYPSE

Rev 1:1—3:22	Prologue and Patmos Vision
Rev 4:1—11:18	The Lamb's Scroll and Its Consequences
Rev 11:19—20:15	The Battle between the Male Child and the Destroyers of the Earth
Rev 21:1—22:21	Salvation: The New Jerusalem and Epilogue

PROLOGUE AND PATMOS VISION (REV 1:1 – 3:22)

Revelation 1:1–8 orients the reader in identifying the hybrid genre of the book. It is a prophecy or communication of God's word (1:3). It draws heavily on the conventions of Jewish apocalypses, narrative accounts of heavenly revelations given to privileged human recipients (1:1–2). It is sent as a circular letter to seven congregations of Jesus believers in the western region of Asia Minor (1:4). Moreover, it is clearly intended to be read aloud to those assembled congregations (1:3), perhaps in the context of eucharistic worship.

The prologue (1:1–3) and letter opening (1:4–8) also introduce some of the key actors. God, the one "who is and who was and who is to come" (1:4), is the implied primary actor, though God will be largely offstage through much of the story. As "the Alpha and the Omega" (1:8), God is the Creator, who continues to sustain his creation, and acts to bring his plan to completion at the end. In the story itself, God acts through his agent Jesus Christ (1:5-6). This whole book is the "revelation of Jesus Christ" (1:1), both because Jesus is the one who reveals, and because he is the content of that revelation. The line of communication of this revelation—from God to Jesus, through his angel "to his servant John," from John to the seven churches—will be important for understanding the structure of Revelation as a whole (e.g., 5:7; 10:1-11).

Beginning at verse 9, John describes his inaugural vision, received while he was on the island called Patmos (1:9). The temporal setting for this vision is "on the Lord's day" (1:10), in other words Sunday, the day of the resurrection. On the day that his fellow believers in the Asian churches gathered for the Eucharist, John sees a heavenly being, the awesome "one like a son of man" (1:12-20). The kaleidoscopic imagery of this vision, our first glimpse of Christ in the book, will be discussed in more detail in chapter 3.

John now describes (2−3) how the son of man dictates a series of seven oracles or prophetic messages, which John is to send to the angels of the seven churches (probably the guardian angels or heavenly representatives of those individual congregations). These are penetrating descriptions of the truth about each congregation, two (Smyrna and Philadelphia) receiving only praise, one (Laodicea) only criticism, the remainder a combination of both. As discussed in the introduction, these messages provide evidence for the social situation of the seven churches. Some followers of Jesus in these small congregations are faithful in their witness, while others are compromised, seduced by the benefits, economic or otherwise, of their surrounding culture.

In the background here is the perennial question of a Christian's relationship with their surrounding culture. How far are Christians called to participate in that culture, functioning as leaven to imbue it with kingdom values (Matt 13:33)? How far should Christians dissociate themselves from it? When must the former give way to the latter? There is a spectrum of views within the NT. The concrete background here is the influence of imperial Rome in the cities of the province of Asia, largely viewed as a positive influence, at least by the urban elites. The influence of Rome had brought economic prosperity and significant honor to several of these cities. Some of them (e.g., Ephesus and Pergamum) were centers of the imperial cult. What Revelation "unveils" (the root meaning of "apocalypse") is the other side of this beneficent empire, its beastly face (see especially Rev 13:1–10).

Before John's main visions begin, therefore, a penetrating spotlight is shone into the heart of the churches. Ironically, many across the centuries have read Revelation as an encoded criticism of their religious or political opponents. Yet Revelation 2–3 presents a church under judgment, praised for its strengths, challenged for its weakness and its compromises, and invited to repent.

THE LAMB'S SCROLL AND ITS CONSEQUENCES (REV 4:1 – 11:18)

The first major scene shift now takes place, as John "was caught up in spirit" (4:2) and granted privileged access to heaven. What he describes is both a heavenly throne room and a heavenly temple. It resembles descriptions of the emperor's court in Rome, the center of earthly power in the world John inhabited. The heavenly throne room will regularly reappear throughout Revelation as the locus of true power and authority in the cosmos, an indictment of rival imperial claims. The throne room is the privileged perspective from which John can view and understand earthly reality correctly. The series of concentric circles (angels, elders, living creatures) converging on the throne of God present a powerful visual scene of heavenly worship.

The heavenly scene is interrupted by the introduction of an unexpected figure, the Lamb (5:6), a second image of Christ that will be explored in detail in chapter 4. This Lamb is worthy to open the scroll, tightly sealed with seven seals, in the hand of the one on the throne. The contents of the scroll are not made explicit, though it seems to contain God's plan to save his people and rescue the world from injustice, chaos, and evil. The execution of this plan, however, requires that the scroll first be opened.

As the Lamb breaks each seal in succession, but before the scroll is fully opened, John witnesses a series of events: the emergence of four horsemen, symbolizing victory, bloodshed, famine, and death, respectively (6:1–8); a vision of slaughtered souls under the altar, crying out for God to act (6:9–11); and a mighty earthquake and other cosmic signs causing human beings to hide (6:12–17). These are the so-called messianic woes — wars, rumors of wars, famines, earthquakes — that were expected to precede the end of this age and the arrival of the messianic kingdom. Such events are anticipated by Jesus in the Synoptic Gospels (Matt 24:3–8; Mark 13:3–8; Luke 21:7–11). That they are each inaugurated here by the opening of the seals reveals that the Lamb has taken control of history, providing meaning to those events that herald salvation. The mention of the souls under the altar indicates that the story of the slaughtered Lamb will be interwoven with the story of the victorious martyrs.

There is, however, a delay between the opening of the sixth and seventh seals, which adds suspense to the narrative. John hears a roll call of soldiers ready to participate in the last battle between God's armies and the enemy: 144,000 male Israelites, twelve thousand from each of Israel's tribes (7:1-8). Yet what he then sees — this army after the battle, after the "time of great distress" — radically revises what he hears. The Lamb's real army comprises males and females, drawn "from every nation, race, people, and tongue" (7:9). It becomes clear that 144,000 is not a literal number, but a symbolic number designating that number "which no one could count" (the square of twelve, a number symbolizing completion, multiplied by a thousand, a biblical number for a great multitude).

The opening of the seventh seal leads to profound silence in heaven "for about half an hour" (8:1). This seventh opening also initiates a new sequence of seven: the blowing of seven trumpets by seven priestly angels (8:6 — 11:18). Trumpets were blown for a variety of reasons in ancient Israel: accompanying worship in the Jerusalem temple, proclaiming fasts, heralding victory in battle, and announcing the Day of the Lord. In the Book of Joshua, seven trumpets were blown by seven priests as the city of Jericho fell to the invading Israelites (Josh 6:1-21). With the blowing of Revelation's seven trumpets, the coming judgment seems to be in view.

But the language is more poetic than literal, with several echoes of the plagues of Egypt that preceded the liberation of God's people at the exodus (Exod 7 — 11). There are also echoes of the first account of creation in Genesis 1, albeit in reverse, as though God's creative act of bringing order out of chaos is being dramatically unravelled. The consequences become increasingly horrific, as in the detailed descriptions of locusts and horses at the fifth and sixth trumpets, ugly and destructive hybrid creatures, part animal, part human, part demonic (Rev 9:1-21). The nightmarish visions reveal the horror of a world in which the emperor rather than God is in control. This world stands under divine judgment. However, they also reveal the promise of a new exodus to liberate God's people from the nightmare, achieved through the collapse of the new Jericho, Rome, and the emergence of a new creation, restoring order out of the chaos, in which the Lamb will play a central role.

As occurred between the sixth and seventh seals, there is a delay between the blowing of the sixth and seven trumpets (10:1 – 11:14). This narrative delay heightens the suspense for the reader, waiting for the end to come. It parallels the experience of the Church, living in the "in-between" time separating Christ's first and second comings, called to remain watchful while Christ's coming is delayed. The delay between the sixth and seventh seals (7:1-17) provided a vision of the Church, an army of warriors before and after "the time of great distress." The Church's vocation is also the focus of this interlude between the sixth and seventh trumpets. Revelation 10 presents the commissioning of John as a prophet, by a "mighty angel" who resembles Christ (and is probably Christ's own angel). He holds "a small scroll that had been opened," perhaps a smaller version of the heavenly scroll opened by the Lamb, which becomes the source of John's prophetic inspiration as he devours its words (10:2, 8-10; cf. 1:1). Revelation 11 presents the Church under the guise of God's temple, measured as God's sacred space and therefore protected by him (11:1-2; cf. Zech 2:5-9), followed by a description of the ministry of two faithful witnesses (Rev 11:3-14). These two witnesses, or "lampstands" (a symbol already used of the churches at Rev 1:20), symbolize the faithful witnessing church (two being the number of witness, Deut 19:15).

Finally, the end arrives when the seventh trumpet is blown (Rev 11:15–18). Paul associated the resurrection of the dead with "the last trumpet" (1 Cor 15:52). Here, too, the final trumpet announces the judgment and arrival of God's kingdom: "The kingdom of the world now belongs to our Lord and to his Anointed, and he will reign forever and ever" (Rev 11:15). The arrival of the end means not only the time for the dead to be judged and God's servants to be rewarded, but the time "to destroy those who destroy the earth" (11:18). It is surprising to find this divine concern for the redemption of the created world in a book so often treated as world-denying.[2]

THE BATTLE BETWEEN THE MALE CHILD AND THE DESTROYERS OF THE EARTH (REV 11:19 – 20:15)

Yet we are only halfway through the book. The reason for this is that the story needs to be told again, this time from the perspective of the church. Or rather, the contents of the scroll revealing God's plan to save the world – in which the Lamb and his churches play a central role – can now be described. So, the Apocalypse takes its readers back to the beginning. There is a new opening in heaven (11:19; the last major section began with an "open door" in heaven, 4:1). The two signs of a glorious, pregnant woman and a dragon/serpent (12:1–6, 13–18) recall the origins of humanity's

---

2. For the theological potential of Revelation for Christian reflection on ecological concerns, see, e.g., Micah D. Kiel, *Apocalyptic Ecology: The Book of Revelation, the Earth, and the Future* (Collegeville, MN: Liturgical Press, 2017).

problem in Genesis 3. But this woman is not only Eve. She also recalls Israel, Mother Zion/Jerusalem, and Mary, the representative of Israel who gave birth to the Messiah (e.g., Gen 37:9; Exod 14:1-31; 19:4; Isa 26:16 – 27:1; Mic 4:10). The dragon is identified as "the ancient serpent, who is called the Devil and Satan" (Rev 12:9), who is intent on destroying the Messiah, but who loses his foothold in heaven, and whose ultimate defeat is connected to the Messiah's death and the faithful witness of his followers (12:11a).

This heavenly vision, then, presents the broad sweep of salvation history, culminating in the "birth" of the woman's male child, despite diabolical attacks. It continues with the "new exodus" brought about by the Messiah, as the woman flees into the wilderness with "the two wings of the great eagle" (12:14; cf. Exod 19:4), and the war waged by the dragon on "the rest of her offspring" (Rev 12:17), members of the church.

Subsequent chapters extend this language of warfare. Cast down to earth, the dragon uses two monstrous surrogates, a beast "come out of the sea" and another "out of the earth," or "from the land," to continue the attacks against the church (13:1-18). The first beast recalls the four beasts emerging from the sea in Daniel 7:1-8, generally understood as the Babylonian, Median, Persian, and Greek empires, who oppressed God's people. John's one beast combines all the worst features of all four. We are best to interpret this beast as a symbol of all oppressive rulers, albeit finding concrete manifestation in John's day in the Roman empire. Its "number" (666, although 616 is also attested) is the numerical value of Nero Caesar, persecutor of Roman Christians, when written in Hebrew letters. The second beast seems to symbolize local elites (whether in the holy land, or, more likely, in the province of Asia) who support the "beastly" characteristics of imperial Rome, politically, religiously, and economically.

The military might of the sea beast seems impregnable enough. But Revelation also describes the opposing army (already alluded to at 12:11). It appears at 14:1-5 as the 144,000 (the Israelite warriors in the military role call of 7:1-8), now with the Lamb on Mount Zion, the "holy mountain" on which God will enthrone his Messiah, from where he will shepherd the nations (Ps 2:6-9). This army reappears at Revelation 15:2-4, standing on the sea of glass, singing "the song of Moses, the servant of God, and the song of the Lamb" (15:3). The replay of the crossing of the sea at the first exodus (Exod 14 – 15) is obvious. Between these two scenes, angels announce the coming judgment, including the fall of the great city Babylon, and John describes a vision of the harvesting of the earth, in which "one who looked like a son of man" plays a key role (Rev 14:6-20).

This story of a new exodus involving the Lamb and his armies intensifies. Seven angels emerge from the heavenly temple, dressed as priests, and pour out the seven last plagues (15:5 – 16:21). The effects of the seven trumpets already recalled the plagues of Egypt that prepared for the first exodus (8:7 – 9:21). The connections between the seven bowls and the Egyptian plagues are even stronger.

The remaining visions of this section of Revelation bring the liberating new exodus to its climax. The announcement of the judgment at the seventh trumpet included the proclamation that the time has come "to destroy those who destroy the earth" (11:18). Revelation 17 – 20 describes the systematic destruction of those destroyers, as the mopping-up operation of the Lamb's victory is completed. First, John is shown the fall of the great city, Babylon, whose demise had been predicted at 14:8. Following ancient convention, the city is first shown personified as a woman, though this woman/city is shockingly unveiled as both a prostitute and a vampire, "drunk on the blood of the holy ones and on the blood of the witnesses to Jesus" (17:6). Feminist critics have rightly drawn our attention to the problematic aspects of this description.

The precise identity of "Babylon" is disputed. A minority of scholars identify this city as historical Jerusalem, who is also called a harlot by the prophets (e.g., Isa 1:21; Jer 13:27; Ezek 16:15–22; 23:1–4). Babylon is seated on the beast because Jerusalem is dependent on and supported by Roman imperial power. More likely, however, Babylon is the city at the center of the beastly empire, Rome. This makes best sense of the statement that Babylon is "the great city that has sovereignty over the kings of the earth" (Rev 17:18). Having described Babylon in detail, Revelation then provides a lengthy response—part taunt, part lament, part celebration—to the city's desolation (18:1—19:8). Having plundered the earth's resources for self-gain, this exploitative city now finds itself in ruins, mourned over by those (merchants, sea captains, client rulers) who benefited from its greatness.

Another vision of Christ, as a warrior riding a white horse, moves the action on (19:11–21; this will be explored in more detail in chapter 5). The warrior with his armies now oversees the destruction of the remaining "destroy[ers of] the earth" (11:18). The ensuing battle leads to the two beasts, now described as "the beast" and "the false prophet," being thrown into "the fiery pool burning with sulfur" (19:20). The dragon is then dealt with, in two stages. First, he is chained and imprisoned in the bottomless pit for a thousand years, like a tamed animal that has lost its power to harm (20:1–3). After his release, he is finally defeated, joining his two lackeys in the lake of fire (20:7–10). In between, we are shown what a Satan-free world looks like, as the resurrected martyrs reign with the Messiah for a thousand years (20:4–6). Finally, as judgment comes for all the dead, these destroyers are joined in the pool of fire by Death and Hades (20:11–15). This chronological sequence is appropriate if we recall Paul's words that the "last enemy to be destroyed is death" (1 Cor 15:26).

SALVATION: THE NEW JERUSALEM AND EPILOGUE (REV 21:1 – 22:21)

Now that the destroyers have been dealt with, John turns to the vision of ultimate salvation. The climax to Revelation's story is a world purged of all that threatens, a "new heaven and a new earth" (21:1; cf. Isa 65:17), and a "new Jerusalem," gifted by God (Rev 21:2). Strikingly, such a world means that "the sea was no more" (21:1), reflecting the biblical view of the sea as symbolizing chaos and danger (it was from the sea that the first beast emerged at 13:1). The big picture is provided in 21:1–8: the descent of the holy city, which is also the Lamb's bride; the assurance that "there shall be no more death or mourning, wailing or pain" (21:4); and God's declaration: "Behold, I make all things new" (21:5).

John then uses a "zoom lens" technique to provide a detailed description of this city (21:9 – 22:5), drawing on a range of OT texts. It is striking that Revelation's vision of ultimate salvation is centered on a city. Cities are places of human community and human culture, built by human endeavor. True, this city is given by God and descends out of heaven to earth. Yet it is still a city, suggesting that our salvation comes not at the expense of human culture, but through transfiguring it. Moreover, cities are places of security, with walls and gates to protect their citizens from external attacks. This makes a city an appropriate symbol for salvation, whose root meaning is rescue or safety.

Nor is this any new city, but the new *Jerusalem*, fulfilling all the hopes and promises of the old Jerusalem. That it is the perfection of all cities is denoted by its dazzling brilliance—reflecting the presence of God and the Lamb (21:23)—and by its perfect proportions. It sits foursquare, with three gates on each of its four sides (twelve in all, a number symbolizing completion or perfection). The wall has "twelve courses of stones as its foundation" (21:14). All its dimensions are multiples of twelve: the measurement of its wall (probably its width) is 144 cubits (twelve multiplied by twelve: 21:17). The city's length, width, and height are "twelve thousand stadia" (21:16, author's translation), again emphasizing that this is the most perfectly proportioned city. NABRE's paraphrase "fifteen hundred miles" (roughly the distance between Washington, D.C., and Denver, or between London and the coast of north Africa) certainly evokes the almost-unimaginable greatness of this city. However, fixation on the literal number risks overlooking its symbolic function as denoting perfection.

Three further dimensions of the New Jerusalem vision are worth noting. First, John's angelic guide shows him "the river of life-giving water" flowing down the middle of the city's street, with "the tree of life" growing on either side of the river (22:1–2). Both these images recall the story of Eden (Gen 2:8–14). The New Jerusalem is a garden city, in which paradise is restored. Second, contemporary readers may miss the full importance of John's statement that "I saw no temple in the city" (Rev 21:22). Few cities in the ancient world would have lacked a temple (indeed, most cities would have had multiple temples, dedicated to dif-

28

ferent gods). The absence of a temple in the New Jerusalem is especially shocking, given that Jerusalem's whole raison d'être was to house God's temple, the locus of God's presence with his people. The reason for its absence is twofold. The presence of God and the Lamb at the heart of the city (21:22) renders a separate temple building unnecessary. As a corollary to this divine presence, John sees no temple *in* the city because the city itself *is* a temple. Its cuboid dimensions mirror the dimensions of the holy of holies in Solomon's original temple (1 Kgs 6:20).

The third point to note is the collapse of Revelation's tripartite cosmology. Earlier in Revelation, John envisaged reality in three tiers: heaven, earth, and the realm under the earth, the latter apparently associated with the sea and the "abyss" or "bottomless pit" (5:3, 13; 7:2; 9:1–2; 11:7; 12:12; 13:1; 14:7; 17:8). In part, this division reflects the apocalyptic idea of certain territory being contested between good and evil. Having been expelled from heaven, the dragon was operative on the earth, particularly through the activities of the two beasts (12:9, 18; 13:4). The realm below the earth was the source of evil and chaos, such as the demonic locusts (9:1–12) or the sea beast (11:7; 17:8). Now, not only has the threatening sea or subterranean water disappeared (21:1); there is no longer any separation between above and below. Heaven has come to earth. God's dwelling is with humanity (21:3). God and the Lamb dwell at the heart of the city (21:22).

All symbols have their limitations, however. The strength of the city image is that it speaks of safety, security, rescue from enemies. It thus befits a vision of the world where all threats to human flourishing have been eliminated, through the destruction of the earth's destroyers. The strength of the temple image is that it envisages a holy people, a priestly people, set apart for the worship of God.

The downside, however, is that both images still presuppose an outside. Therefore, this final vision still speaks of outsiders: "nothing unclean will enter it, nor any[one] who does abominable things or tells lies" (21:27); "outside are the dogs, the sorcerers, the unchaste, the murderers, the idol-worshipers, and all who love and practice deceit" (22:15). Such language jars, in a vision of "a new heaven and a new earth" that should have been purged of all outsider threats. Even apocalyptic symbols only take us so far.

The book concludes with an epilogue (22:6–21), paralleling the prologue (1:1–8). It brings the reader back from the visionary world to terra firma. The reader returns with John to Patmos (1:9). More importantly, the reader is back in the worshiping community, a reminder that the intervening visions were designed to be read aloud by a reader to the assembled congregations (1:3). A chorus of different voices interject, only some of which can be identified (the interpreting angel, Jesus, the Spirit, the bridal church). These voices inject a sense of urgency: "Behold, I am coming soon" (22:7, 12, 20). "Do not seal up the prophetic words of this book, for the appointed time is near" (22:10). "The Spirit and the bride say, 'Come'" (22:17). The hearers are to take to heart the message of this book (which is set on a par with the Mosaic Torah as divine revelation: Rev 22:18–19; cf. Deut 4:2) and keep the vision alive by making the church's urgent prayer their own: "Amen! Come, Lord Jesus!" (Rev 22:20).

CHAPTER TWO

Titles of Christ in Revelation

The Apocalypse ends with an urgent prayer: "Amen! Come, Lord Jesus!" (Rev 22:20). But what does the book reveal about this Lord Jesus? To answer this question requires a multipronged approach. Certainly, the titles John attributes to Jesus (e.g., Messiah; Son of God; the Lamb) play a significant role. Yet recent study of NT Christology highlights the limitations of focusing only on christological titles (a so-called Titular Christology).[1] Other aspects also provide crucial insights into how, for example, Matthew or Luke or Paul understands who Christ is and what he has done for us.

For example, NT books often contain subtle allusions to OT characters, detectable only through careful reading. To take one example, Matthew's Gospel frequently presents Jesus in ways that recall Israel's greatest leader, Moses (e.g., Matt 2:16-18; 5−7; 17:2; cf. Exod 1:15−2:10; 34:1-26, 29-35). All this is presented subtly, without explicit mention of Moses's name. In other cases, NT writers evoke the great narratives of Israel's past. In all three Synoptic Gospels, the juxtaposition of Christ's baptism with his temptation in the wilderness recall Israel's crossing the sea and entry into

---

1. For example, Frank J. Matera, *New Testament Christology* (Louisville, KY: Westminster John Knox, 1999).

the wilderness of Sinai (Matt 3:13 – 4:11; Mark 1:9-13; Luke 3:21 – 4:13; cf. Exod 14 – 16).

Moreover, in a narrative text, the characterization of Jesus in the story is crucial to a rounded understanding of its author's Christology. Jesus's character traits, his relationship with his Father, and his salvific role are gradually revealed through what Jesus says, how Jesus acts, and how other characters and character groups respond to him within the story (a "narrative Christology").

All this applies to understanding Revelation's portrait of Jesus. First, the Christ of the Apocalypse conforms to certain OT categories, without explicit titles being cited (e.g., the Divine Warrior). Second, we have already seen how Revelation evokes multiple narratives from Israel's past that also illuminate its portrayal of Jesus. Most notable is Revelation's tale of a new exodus, which pervades the whole book. But Revelation alludes to other stories too. It invites compromised believers in the seven churches to come out of Babylon (Rev 18:4), recalling the prophecy of Deutero-Isaiah (the sixth-century BCE prophet responsible for Isa 40 – 55) concerning the return from exile. In Revelation's case, the destination is not the old but the *new* Jerusalem (chaps. 21 – 22).

Third, the overview of Revelation's story in chapter 1 has already suggested that narrative Christology is as important for John of Patmos as for the four evangelists. The readers of Revelation learn who Jesus is through how his character develops. He is the key actor, orchestrating events that culminate in the salvation of God's people. We periodically hear Jesus's voice (most extensively in chaps. 2 – 3, where Jesus dictates to John a series of seven oracles or messages). Other characters react to Jesus in different ways, whether through faith and worship, or opposition and open warfare. As in the Gospels, the plot is a story of conflict, in which characters line up either for or against Jesus, and audiences are challenged to make a similar decision.

But Revelation's story world is also quite different from the story world of the Gospels. Whereas in the latter, Jesus is engaged for the most part in everyday actions and encounters (teaching, healing, debating, sharing meals), in the Apocalypse he appears in symbolic visions, which are harder to interpret. Moreover, given the fluid, kaleidoscopic character of Revelation's imagery, Christ appears under different guises, each of which contributes an important facet of this mysterious Lord. Subsequent chapters will examine the most important of these guises. Some use explicit titles (e.g., the Lamb), or nontitular descriptions (e.g., "one like a son of man"; the male child). Others are more implicit, conforming Jesus to existing roles or categories (e.g., Christ as the high priest). The sheer diversity of these images reminds us of the multifaceted character of Revelation's Christ, his role in God's plan, and the consequences of his saving death and resurrection.

Before proceeding to these central images, this chapter will consider additional titles ascribed to Jesus in the Apocalypse, some of which are mentioned only fleetingly. Despite their infrequency, each plays a role in our overall understanding. This chapter will also include a brief discussion of what Revelation's Jesus says, to complete the picture of what he does, and what is said about him.

JESUS AS ISRAEL'S MESSIAH

The Apocalypse breathes the air of early Christian Judaism. Although it envisages a church gathered "from every nation, race, people, and tongue" (Rev 7:9), its main categories for describing Jesus reflect the Jewish roots of the movement that would become Christianity. Whether

Revelation in its present form was written in the late 60s or mid 90s of the first century CE, it echoes the convictions of Jesus's earliest Jewish followers.

"Christ" ("Messiah" or "Anointed," Greek *Christos*) is one of the most popular titles of Jesus throughout the NT. Its roots lie in the Jewish conviction that God would raise up an anointed figure in the last days, as his agent for salvation: normally a king (e.g., Pss. Sol. 17), though a dual expectation of a priestly Messiah and a royal Messiah is also found (e.g., 1QS 9:11). However, scholars often observe how, in much of the NT, *Christos* has become almost a second name for Jesus: "Jesus Christ" or, less frequently, "Christ Jesus" (e.g., Matt 1:1; Mark 1:1; 1 Cor 1:1–3).

This combination "Jesus Christ" is found in Revelation's opening verses (1:1, 2, 5). More striking, however, are the remaining four occurrences of *Christos*, which retain the older sense of God's chosen "Anointed" or Messiah. The blowing of the seventh trumpet leads to the proclamation that "the kingdom of the world now belongs to our Lord and to his Anointed, and he will reign forever and ever" (11:15). A transition has now taken place in history, in which the kingdom of God has been established over rival claimants to the throne, and the Messiah shares in God's rule. A similar claim is made in the heavenly canticle in Revelation 12, which provides a "running commentary" on the expulsion of Satan and his angels from heaven, connecting that expulsion with the deaths of the Lamb and the martyrs:

> Now have salvation and power come,
>> and the kingdom of our God
>> and the authority of his Anointed. (12:10)

The final two references to the Messiah occur in the short passage describing the so-called millennium (or thousand-year reign of the martyrs with Christ). The significance is somewhat obscured in the NABRE translation, which speaks of the resurrected as reigning "with Christ" for a thousand years, and of becoming "priests of God and of Christ" (20:4, 6). In both cases, the Greek has the definite article: "the Messiah" or "the Anointed" (*ho Christos*). Jesus retains his role as God's anointed agent through whom God's kingdom or reign is established.

Jewish messianic hopes are also evident in a double title given to the Lamb in the heavenly vision of Revelation 4–5. One of the elders reassures the weeping John that "the lion of the tribe of Judah, the root of David, has triumphed, enabling him to open the scroll with its seven seals" (5:5). This description interweaves two OT passages, Jacob's blessing of Judah, ancestor of King David, and Isaiah's prophecy of the ideal Davidic king emerging from the root of David's father Jesse (Gen 49:9; Isa 11:1). More will be said about these messianic titles and their relationship to Christ as the Lamb in chapter 4.

At the very end of the book, the exalted Jesus reprises his earlier identification as "the root of David," and adds an additional title: "I am the root and offspring of David, the bright morning star" (Rev 22:16; cf. 2:28). Christ, shining in glory, is likened to Venus, the original morning star (a similar claim, albeit using a different Greek phrase, is made at 2 Pet 1:19). There is probably an allusion here to Balaam's oracle about a star arising from Jacob (Num 24:17), read by some first-century Jews as a prophecy of the royal Messiah (e.g., 4QTest 9–13). In the Testament of Judah (probably a Jewish text reworked by early Christians), Balaam's star prophecy is also combined with Isaiah's oracle about the root of Jesse (T. Jud. 24:1).

BALAAM'S PROPHECY

> I see him, though not now;
> I observe him, though not near:
> A star shall advance from Jacob,
> and a scepter shall rise from Israel. (Num 24:17)

And after this a star will come forth for you out of Jacob in peace, and a man will arise from among my descendants like the sun of righteousness, living with men in meekness and righteousness, and no sin will be found in him....

> Then will the sceptre of my kingdom shine forth,
> And from your root will come a stem. (T. Jud. 24:1, 5;
> trans. M. de Jonge in Sparks)[2]

A final echo of Jewish messianism appears in the introduction to the message to the angel of the Thyatiran church: "The Son of God, whose eyes are like a fiery flame and whose feet are like polished brass" (Rev 2:18). Son of God is an important title of Jesus in the NT (see Matt 4:3; 8:29; 27:54; Mark 1:1; Luke 1:35; John 1:34; Acts 9:20; Rom 1:4; Gal 2:20; Heb 4:14; 1 John 3:8). Surprisingly, it is only used here in Revelation (though Christ does speak elsewhere of God as his Father, e.g., 1:6; 2:28; 3:5, 21). "Son of God" did not necessarily have connotations of divinity for first-century Jews. It expressed a special relationship with God, and could be used of angels (e.g., Gen 6:2; Job 1:6), the people of Israel collectively (e.g., Hos 11:1), a pious Israelite (e.g., Wis 2:13–18), Israel's king (e.g., Pss 2:7; 89:27), and the royal Messiah (e.g., 4Q246; 4 Ezra 7:28).

---

2. English translations of Jewish pseudepigrapha in this book are taken from H. F. D. Sparks, ed., *The Apocryphal Old Testament* (Oxford: Clarendon Press, 1984).

The strong allusions to Psalm 2 in Revelation 2:18–29 (including a near quotation of Ps 2:8–9 in vv. 26–27) gives priority to the royal, messianic connotations of Son of God. Psalm 2 will be reused to describe Jesus's messianic role later in the Apocalypse (12:5; 19:15). Nonetheless, "Son of God" is combined here with more exalted images that point to Jesus as being more than a human Messiah: eyes "like a fiery flame" and feet "like polished brass." Jewish messianism provides the categories, but these are reworked to express early Christian conviction of Christ's unique relationship to God.

JESUS AS WITNESS

The story of the Apocalypse presupposes the wider story of Jesus. Almost nothing is said explicitly about Jesus's earthly life, teaching, or public ministry: there is an ambiguous reference to his "birth" (12:5), and one mention of his "twelve apostles" (21:14). However, early Christian familiarity with the wider story of Jesus lies in the background.[3] Later, we will explore how Revelation presents, albeit in symbolic form, Christ's passion, death, and resurrection. But the backstory of Jesus's earthly life is also implied in the repeated phrase "the testimony of Jesus" or "the testimony of Jesus Christ." This phrase occurs six times in the book (1:2, 9; 12:17; 19:10 [twice]; 20:4).

Testimony, or witness, is a key concept in the Apocalypse, as also in the Gospel of John, with which Revelation has traditionally been paired (e.g., John 1:7–8, 15, 19; 2:25; 5:31–39; 18:37; 19:35; 21:24). We also hear of the souls under

---

3. For a good discussion, see M. Eugene Boring, "Narrative Christology in the Apocalypse," *CBQ* 54 (1992): 702–23.

the altar, who were killed "because of the witness they bore" (Rev 6:9), and the "testimony" of the two witnesses, or *martyres* (11:7). The prominence of this concept is evident from John's self-introduction as the one who "gives witness to the word of God and to the testimony of Jesus Christ by reporting what he saw" (Rev 1:2).

The "testimony of Jesus" (Greek *martyria Iēsou*) is ambiguous. It could refer to the witness that others bear to Jesus, in preaching and in the pattern of their lives. But it could also mean the witness that Jesus himself bore, to the truth of God, which is to be emulated by his followers. The primary focus seems to be on Jesus's own testimony. For Revelation, Jesus is the witness par excellence. This conviction is expressed by several titles. He is "the faithful witness" (1:5), or, in his own words, "the faithful and true [*or* trustworthy] witness" (3:14). This will be reprised in the vision of Christ the Divine Warrior, riding a white horse, who is called "Faithful and True" (19:11). He is also "the Amen" (3:14), a transliteration of the Hebrew word meaning "truly" or "surely" (in Isa 65:16, God is called "the God of Amen," i.e., the one who can be relied upon to keep his word). Christ is the reliable witness, who speaks the truth, keeps his word, and in so doing reveals the truth about the world.

THE EFFECTS OF JESUS'S DEATH AND RESURRECTION

Jesus is preeminently witness to the truth in his passion and death. The First Letter to Timothy describes how Christ "gave testimony under Pontius Pilate" (1 Tim 6:13) during his passion. Similarly, the Apocalypse sees a strong connection between the testimony of Jesus and his death and resurrection. As faithful witness, he is "the firstborn of the dead and ruler of the kings of the earth" (Rev 1:5). However, in Revelation's symbolic visions, the story of Christ's passion, death, and resurrection reads very differently from the passion narratives of the Gospels, particularly the Synoptics.

Subsequent chapters will explore Revelation's symbolic reinterpretation of Christ's passion in more detail. Preeminent is the key character of the slaughtered Lamb, killed but victorious, and worthy of worship (chap. 5). The effects of Christ's death and resurrection will also be presented in the unfamiliar guise of the warrior Christ, riding on a white horse against his enemies (19:11–16). But they are also hinted at by the opening description of Christ just cited (1:5).

First, Jesus is "the firstborn of the dead" (see also Col 1:18). That Christ is "the firstborn" is commonplace in the NT (e.g., Luke 2:7; Rom 8:29; Heb 1:6). But the phrase here understands Christ's death to be a "birth," such that Christ is now "the firstborn of the dead." By his death and resurrection, a new humanity has come to birth. As the elder son, he is the first of many who will also participate in the resurrection from the dead.

Second, he is now "ruler of the kings of the earth." Throughout the OT, the "kings of the earth" are pagan rulers (e.g., 1 Kgs 10:23; Pss 102:16; 138:4; Isa 24:21; 1 Macc 1:2). Christ might not look much like a ruler, still less a ruler of Gentile monarchs, the Roman emperor included. A dying man, rejected by the leaders of his people, deserted by most of his closest followers, and subjected to the humiliating Roman penalty of crucifixion, appears the antithesis of the Lord of glory. Yet, paradoxically, universal kingship is one consequence of his death. The whole Apocalypse could be understood as the unveiling of Christ's sovereign rule, his victory over his rivals through power manifest in weakness.

The juxtaposition of these last two titles — firstborn of the dead; ruler of the kings of the earth — might have been suggested by Psalm 89: "I myself make him the firstborn, Most High over the kings of the earth" (v. 28). For the Psalmist, the Lord is speaking here about his servant David. John of Patmos reads this psalm messianically, as a reference to Jesus as David's Son, the "root of David."

Closely related is the title "Lord of lords and king of kings" (Rev 17:14), also found in the form "King of kings and Lord of lords" (19:16). The early Christians associated the acclamation of Jesus as Lord with his resurrection, whereby he was exalted to God's right hand (Ps 110:1; see Acts 2:34–35; 1 Cor 15:25; Heb 1:13). Revelation's extended title is probably influenced by the Greek version of Daniel 4:37, where God is acclaimed as "God of gods and Lord of lords and King of kings." A title of God is now transferred to the exalted Christ.

THE PREEXISTENT CHRIST

This transfer of divine titles to the exalted Jesus of Nazareth is a striking feature of John's Apocalypse and will be discussed further in chapter 6. Equally striking are titles that connect Christ to protology, that is, theological reflection on the world's origins. The first example is initially presented as a divine title: "I am the Alpha and the Omega" (1:8). These two letters, the *A* to *Z* of the Greek alphabet (corresponding to the aleph and taw of the Hebrew alphabet), speak of God as both the Creator of the cosmos and the goal toward which the historical process is moving. The NT scholar Richard Bauckham observes that this title may be derived from Jewish speculation about God's name YHWH, sometimes transliterated into Greek as IAΩ, in other words, containing the letters alpha and omega.[4] The same point is conveyed by "the beginning and the end" (added to "I am the Alpha and the Omega" at Rev 21:6). This formula, drawn from Greek philosophy, was applied to Israel's God by the first-century Jewish apologist Josephus (*Ant.* 8.280).

Both divine titles are also claimed by Christ, who adds a third synonymous title: "I am the Alpha and the Omega, *the first and the last,* the beginning and the end" (22:13; cf. 1:17). Jewish readers would hear echoes of Isaiah 44:6, where God declares, "I am the first, I am the last; there is no God but me" (cf. Isa 41:4; 48:12). Christ was in the beginning, and his coming at the end is to be regarded as the anticipated coming of God.

The second example also focuses on Christ's presence at the beginning of all things. In the message to the angel of the Laodicean church, Christ describes himself as "the origin" or "beginning [*archē*] of God's creation" (Rev 3:14, author's translation). The background to this title is Israel's Wisdom tradition (e.g., Prov 8:22–23), which personified Wisdom as the agent of God's creation, a poetic way of saying that God created wisely. Wisdom Christology is found in several places in the NT (e.g., John 1:1–3; 1 Cor 8:6; Heb 1:2), speaking of Christ's protological role as agent of creation. Interestingly, the only other NT description of Christ as *archē* occurs in the famous christological hymn in Paul's Letter to the Colossians (Col 1:18; the same holds for the phrase "firstborn of the dead," Rev 1:5). Colossae was only ten miles from Laodicea in the Lycus Valley east of Ephesus, suggesting that this title may have been commonplace among Christians in that area.

---

4. Richard Bauckham, *The Theology of the Book of Revelation*, New Testament Theology (Cambridge: Cambridge University Press, 1993), 25–28.

CHRIST AS "BEGINNING" (*ARCHĒ*)

To the angel of the church in Laodicea, write this:
"The Amen, the faithful and true witness, the
source [*archē*] of God's creation, says this."
(Rev 3:14)

He is the image of the invisible God,
the firstborn of all creation....
He is the head of the body, the church.
He is the beginning [*archē*], the firstborn from the dead,
that in all things he himself might be preeminent.
(Col 1:15, 18)

The LORD begot me, the beginning of his works,
the forerunner of his deeds of long ago;
From of old I was formed,
at the first, before the earth. (Prov 8:22–23)

THE VOICE OF JESUS

We began this chapter by noting that, in NT narratives, the characterization of Jesus is important for understanding the text's Christology, alongside explicit titles and implicit OT narratives. Characterization includes what characters say as well as what they do, or what is said about them. Revelation also shapes the readers' perception of Jesus by allowing him to speak for himself. However, given the book's visionary character, it is not always clear when Jesus is the speaker.

Perhaps the clearest example is provided by the seven messages of Revelation 2–3. Though often called seven letters, these are prophetic oracles spoken by the risen Jesus

(1:19; 2:1, etc.), underscoring his divine authority. Just as God's voice is heard in the words of Israel's prophets, in Revelation the exalted Christ speaks divine words of comfort and challenge to the angels of the seven congregations. The repeated "says this" (Greek *tade legei*, 2:1, 8, 12, 18; 3:1, 7, 14) is equivalent to the OT "Thus says the Lord" (Greek *tade legei*, e.g., 1 Kgs 11:31; Isa 1:24; Jer 2:2; Amos 1:6; Mic 2:3).

Christ's words are therefore presented as inspired prophecy, mediated through his prophet John (Rev 1:19). We know from Paul that words of the Lord were uttered by early Christian prophets in the liturgical assembly (1 Cor 14:1-5, 26-33). Revelation 2−3 may have a similar origin. What complicates matters, however, is the repeated phrase "Whoever has ears ought to hear" (Rev 2:7, 11, 17, 29; 3:6, 13, 22; 13:9), which is regularly found on the lips of Jesus in the Synoptic Gospels (e.g., Matt 13:9, 43; Mark 4:9, 23; Luke 8:8). In the complex writing process, traditional sayings of Jesus and ecstatic prophetic utterances may well have been interwoven.

Christ's divine voice is also heard in several "I am" sayings, a feature the Apocalypse shares with John's Gospel. In the Gospel, John's Jesus frequently uses "I am" with a predicate, to explicate different dimensions of his role, and the salvation he offers: "I am the bread of life" (John 6:35); "I am the good shepherd" (John 10:11); "I am the way and the truth and the life" (John 14:6); "I am the true vine" (John 15:1). Similar sayings are found in other religious traditions, to express divine revelation (e.g., "I am Isis, ruler of every land").

In the Apocalypse, "I am" sayings with a predicate are found on the lips of both God and Christ. We have already noted the transfer of "I am the Alpha and the Omega" from the one on the throne (Rev 1:8; 21:6) to Jesus (22:13; cf. 1:17). Christ's final "I am" saying, rich in messianic imagery, has also been discussed above (22:16). In addition, Christ says

43

to the angel of the church in Thyatira, "I am the searcher of hearts and minds" (2:23). Again, this phrase was previously used of Israel's God (Jer 11:20), underscoring the close relationship between Jesus and the one seated on the throne.

I AM Sayings Spoken by God

> "I am the Alpha and the Omega" (1:8).
> "I [am] the Alpha and the Omega, the beginning and the end" (21:6).

I AM Sayings Spoken by Christ

> "I am the first and the last" (1:17).
> "I am the searcher of hearts and minds" (2:23).
> "I am the Alpha and the Omega, the first and the last, the beginning and the end" (22:13).
> "I am the root and offspring of David, the bright morning star" (22:16).

Less certain are unspecified voices that regularly interject themselves into the narrative. We hear, for example, of a voice coming from the four horns of the altar (9:13), or a voice from heaven commanding John to seal up the seven thunders (10:4). At least some of these anonymous interjections appear to come from the voice of Christ. The "trumpetlike voice" inviting John to come up to heaven (4:1) is the same voice spoken when John encountered "one like a son of man" at 1:10–12. The interjection at 16:15 ("Behold, I am coming like a thief") must also be Christ's voice. Not only has a similar saying been spoken by the son of man to the church in Sardis (3:3). It is found on the lips of Jesus in the Gospels (Matt 24:43–44; Luke 12:39–40), and functions in two NT letters as a warning about preparedness for Christ's coming (1 Thess 5:2; 2 Pet 3:10). In Revelation, it interrupts a narrative description of the last battle at Armageddon, like a prophetic oracle. Again, Christ speaks as the divine Christ, through John his prophetic mouthpiece.

Finally, the voice of Jesus is heard three times in the final chapter, each speaking of his final coming. Though God has been described as the one who is coming (Rev 1:4), Christ's expected coming as judge has also been anticipated multiple times (e.g., 1:7; 3:3, 11). His promise is therefore reprised at Revelation 22:7 and 12: "Behold, I am coming soon." Again, the speaker's identity is not given, but the third occurrence in verse 20 removes any doubt: "The one who gives this testimony says, 'Yes, I am coming soon.' Amen! Come, Lord Jesus!"

SUMMARY

Though christological titles and related phrases are only part of the overall picture, their use throughout the Apocalypse contributes significantly to understanding the Christ of the Apocalypse. Some locate Revelation's Jesus firmly in the expectations of Judaism concerning the royal Davidic Messiah. Others tap into the wider story of Jesus familiar to early Christians: his powerful testimony to the truth, and especially the transformative effects of his death and resurrection. But we also find evidence for deeper reflection on Jesus, as not only fully human, but also on the heavenly side of the heaven/earth divide. As well as language of preexistence, influenced by Israel's Wisdom tradition, Christ is described in terms hitherto reserved for Israel's God. This is underscored by the words of Revelation's Jesus, placed on a par with God's prophetic word.

CHAPTER THREE

The Exalted Son of Man

Revelation's first detailed description of Jesus occurs in its opening chapter. John describes how, on the island of Patmos, he received a vision of "one like a son of man," commanding him to write down what he saw (Rev 1:9–11, 13). The mysterious figure then dictated a series of seven messages, one to each of the angels of the seven churches of Asia (chaps. 2—3). Though John's heavenly visitor is unnamed, it gradually becomes clear that he is Christ himself. This chapter will explore this complex vision in some detail to discover what it contributes to the overall Christology of the Apocalypse. It begins with some background information: locating this passage against the backdrop of similar visionary passages in the OT and other Jewish writings.

Vision reports in Jewish and Christian apocalypses often have a distinctive opening. A statement, in the first person, of the visionary's geographical location, indicates that a vision, dream, or heavenly journey is about to occur. In the Book of Daniel, for example, Daniel notes how "I was on the bank of the great river, the Tigris," before describing a vision of "a man dressed in linen" (Dan 10:4–5, 14; cf. 8:16; 9:21). This "man" is certainly a divine messenger, revealing to Daniel what is to happen to God's people "in the last days." The prophet Ezekiel describes how he was by another river in Babylonia, the Chebar, when the heavens opened, and he received visions of God (Ezek 1:1). A similar opening occurs in 4 Ezra (2 Esdras 3 – 14), a Jewish apocalypse roughly contemporaneous with Revelation. Attributed to Ezra, the fifth-century BCE scribe who returned to Jerusalem after the Babylonian exile in the sixth century, 4 Ezra is one Jewish response to the traumatic destruction of Jerusalem and the temple by Rome, the new Babylon, in 70 CE. The author introduces a vision of the angel Uriel by locating the seer at home in bed (4 Ezra 3:1). The common features are (a) specific time reference, (b) use of the first person (sometimes with the seer's name), and (c) named terrestrial location.

In other words, within time, and in a specific place, the veil separating heaven and earth becomes very thin. Heavenly emissaries reveal themselves. Earthly locations become gateways onto eternity. Sometimes, the places are already sacred (e.g., Isaiah's famous vision in the temple, Isa 6). Frequently, however, it is in mundane places (a river, a house, a bed) that earth and heaven coincide.

INTRODUCTIONS TO VISION REPORTS

"In the thirtieth year, on the fifth day of the fourth
  month, while I was among the exiles by the river
  Chebar, the heavens opened, and I saw divine visions"
  (Ezek 1:1).
"In those days, I, Daniel, mourned three full weeks. I ate
  no savory food, took no meat or wine, and did not
  anoint myself at all until the end of the three weeks.
  On the twenty-fourth day of the first month I was on
  the bank of the great river, the Tigris. As I looked up,
  I saw a man dressed in linen with a belt of fine gold
  around his waist" (Dan 10:2-5).

"In the thirtieth year after the destruction of the city,
    I was in Babylon—I, Salathiel, who am also called Ezra.
    I was troubled as I lay on my bed, and my thoughts
    welled up in my heart, because I saw the desolation of
    Zion and the wealth of those who lived in Babylon"
    (4 Ezra [2 Esdras] 3:1-2 NRSV).

A VISION ON THE ISLAND CALLED PATMOS

Similarly, John introduces his first vision with an auto-biographical statement concerning his geographical location (in the first person, with a specific location and time reference):

I, John, your brother, who share with you the distress, the kingdom, and the endurance we have in Jesus, found myself on the island called Patmos because I proclaimed God's word and gave testimony to Jesus. I was caught up in spirit on the Lord's day and heard behind me a voice as loud as a trumpet. (Rev 1:9-10)

This brief opening statement is rich in content. First, John establishes solidarity with his first audiences, and, across the centuries, with all readers or hearers of the Apocalypse. Whatever authority John holds, he and his fellow believers stand before God on an equal footing. He shares with them both the joys and the sorrows of following Christ. John uses the evocative Greek term *sunkoinōnos*: "fellow participant," "cosharer," one who shares communion (*koinōnia*) with others. This cosharing includes "distress" or "tribulation," probably not official Roman persecution, but more indirect hardships experienced by those who follow Christ. This calls for "endurance," "steadfastness," or "perseverance." But John also shares with his fellow believers in "the kingdom" or the "royal rule" of God.

Having established solidarity with his readers, John then asserts his privileged status. He has been the recipient of divine revelation, received "on the Lord's day," the day of the resurrection when early Christians gathered for worship. The terrestrial location for this revelation was "the island called Patmos." Patmos is rarely mentioned in antiquity, and never elsewhere in the Bible. But archaeology and inscriptions show that it had a thriving population, with a rich religious and cultural life. The island itself was dedicated to the goddess Artemis, whose temple dominated the skyline. There is no evidence, despite the frequent claims of scholars, that at the time of John, the Romans used this small, rocky island as a penal colony for criminals.

The precise reason for John's presence on Patmos remains uncertain. However, the wider biblical tradition sheds other light on the meaning of John's words. In the OT, "the islands" were associated with the Gentiles, and located on the margins of the Jewish world, for which Jerusalem was the "navel" of the earth (Ezek 38:12; Josephus, *War* 3.3.5). Patmos, therefore, was for John a Gentile place, far from Jerusalem, as the rivers Chebar and Tigris had been for Ezekiel and Daniel. It is often in the most unlikely locations that heaven reaches to earth.

ANGELOMORPHIC CHRISTOLOGY

The similarity between Revelation's opening vision of Jesus and descriptions of angelic appearances in the OT and other Jewish writings is striking. We have just noted Daniel's vision of a man in linen, generally identified as the angel Gabriel (Dan 10:5–6; cf. 8:16; 9:21). This reflects the tendency in the apocalypses to describe angels in human form. Daniel 10 provides part of the imagery for what John now sees. But the primary influence comes from Daniel's more famous vision of "one like a son a man" (Dan 7:13), the very phrase John uses in Revelation 1:13. In this context, "one like a son of man" is not a title, but a description: a figure who is like a human being. In Daniel, it describes a heavenly being, perhaps the archangel Michael as the heavenly guardian of God's people Israel, appearing in human form. This heavenly figure is brought before the Ancient of Days, God seated on a throne, and given "dominion, splendor, and kingship" (Dan 7:14).

THE DANIELIC SON OF MAN

As the visions during the night continued, I saw
   coming with the clouds of heaven
One like a son of man.
When he reached the Ancient of Days
and was presented before him,
He received dominion, splendor, and kingship;
all nations, peoples, and tongues will serve him.
His dominion is an everlasting dominion
that shall not pass away,
his kingship, one that shall not be destroyed.
   (Dan 7:13–14)

Like Daniel, John sees "one like a son of man" (cf. Dan 7:13; 8:15), a heavenly being appearing in human form. But this figure is no mere angel. His subsequent words identify him as the exalted Jesus: "Do not be afraid. I am the first and the last, the one who lives. Once I was dead, but now I am alive forever and ever" (Rev 1:17b–18a). This is the crucified and risen One, coming to John on Patmos as he first appeared to his disciples after his resurrection in Jerusalem and Galilee.

Scholars often use the term *angelomorphic Christology* to describe this vision. *Angelomorphic* is derived from the Greek, meaning "in angelic form." This is a way of speaking about Jesus that draws upon Jewish traditions about exalted angels who mediate God's presence. Christ is more than an angel; yet speaking of him in terms drawn from Jewish angelology emphasizes his heavenly character, and his ability to reveal God.

The subtle identification of this heavenly being as the risen Christ, who was dead but is now "alive forever and ever" (1:18), is typical of how John writes. He rarely makes explicit, but gradually reveals. This opening vision is like a kaleidoscope, in which diverse OT images combine to build up the first picture of Revelation's Jesus. The pattern constantly changes, as the mind struggles to visualize what is being described. John's description moves swiftly from clothing, to face, to feet, to voice. To appreciate this vision and its rhetorical power requires a vivid imagination.

It is important to recognize the biblical sources for these various images. But what John describes is more than the sum of its parts. They are now reconfigured into a new pattern, which has its own powerful rhetorical effect on the reader, or the audience hearing this passage read in a communal setting.

LOCATION AND CLOTHING

John begins by describing the location and clothing of the heavenly figure: "Then I turned to see whose voice it was that spoke to me, and when I turned, I saw seven gold lampstands and in the midst of the lampstands one like a son of man, wearing an ankle-length robe, with a gold sash around his chest" (Rev 1:12–13). There are clear similarities here with the angel that Daniel saw by the river Tigris. Daniel's human-like figure is dressed in linen, and wears "a belt of fine gold around his waist" (Dan 10:5).

John is more specific. Christ wears "an ankle-length robe" (Greek *podērēs*, literally "reaching to the feet"). Scholars dispute its precise significance, since the term could describe the clothing of a variety of high-ranking officials. However, one plausible proposal is that John alludes to the garment worn by Israel's high priest (e.g., Exod 28:4; Wis 18:24; Sir 45:8). This interpretation is found as early as Irenaeus in the late second century CE:

> For in these words He sets forth something of the glory [which He has received] from His Father, as [where He makes mention of] the head; something in reference to the priestly office also, as in the case of the long garment reaching to the feet. And this was the reason why Moses vested the high priest after this fashion. (*Adv. Haer.* 4.20.11)[1]

This priestly interpretation is strengthened by Christ's location in the midst of seven gold lampstands or menorahs, symbolizing the seven churches (Rev 1:20). This is temple

---

1. English translation from Alexander Roberts, James Donaldson, and A. Cleveland Coxe, ed., *Ante-Nicene Fathers*, vol. 1 (Buffalo, NY: Christian Literature Publishing, 1885), https://www.newadvent.org/fathers/0103420.htm.

imagery (Exod 25:31–40): the risen Lord stands in the midst of his temple community. Thus, Revelation shares with the Letter to the Hebrews the conviction that Christ has become the great high priest (e.g., Heb 7:1–8:6). Like Israel's high priest, Christ's role is bidirectional: he represents God to the people, as mediator, and the people to God, as intercessor.

COMPARISON OF DANIEL 10 AND REVELATION 1

On the twenty-fourth day of the first month I was on the bank of the great river, the Tigris. As I looked up, I saw a man dressed in linen with a belt of fine gold around his waist. His body was like chrysolite, his face shone like lightning, his eyes were like fiery torches, his arms and feet looked like burnished bronze, and the sound of his voice was like the roar of a multitude. I alone, Daniel, saw the vision; but great fear seized those who were with me; they fled and hid themselves, although they did not see the vision. So I was left alone to see this great vision. No strength remained in me; I turned the color of death and was powerless. When I heard the sound of his voice, I fell face forward unconscious. (Dan 10:4–9)

Then I turned to see whose voice it was that spoke to me, and when I turned, I saw seven gold lampstands and in the midst of the lampstands one like a son of man, wearing an ankle-length robe, with a gold sash around his chest. The hair of his head was as white as white wool or as snow, and his eyes were like a fiery flame. His feet were like polished brass refined in a furnace, and his voice was like the sound of rushing water. In his right hand he held seven stars. A sharp two-edged sword

came out of his mouth, and his face shone like the
sun at its brightest. When I caught sight of him, I
fell down at his feet as though dead. (Rev 1:12–17a)

HEAD AND BODY

The parallels with Gabriel in Daniel 10 continue in the
description of Christ's appearance. The head, especially the
face, is the most "personal" part of the human body. We
recognize one another by our faces. The expression of the
face also conveys a person's mood, and their eyes provide
a window into their character (cf. Matt 6:22–23). It is unsurprising, therefore, that John's description returns regularly
to the head: Christ's hair; his eyes; his voice; his mouth. His
head and hair were "as white as white wool or as snow"
(Rev 1:14). John literally writes "as white as wool, which
is white as snow," piling simile upon simile to describe the
divine in terms of the human. White hair denotes great age,
pointing to Christ's eternal character. But more specifically,
John's description merges Daniel's "one like a son of man"
with his "Ancient of Days," whose "clothing was white as
snow, the hair on his head like pure wool" (Dan 7:9). Again,
John alludes to Christ's divinity. The Son of Man bears the
features of God seated on the throne.

Like Daniel's man by the river, John's description continues to emphasize the dazzling, glorious appearance of
Christ. His eyes are "like a fiery flame," and his feet "like
polished brass refined in a furnace" (Rev 1:14–15; cf. Dan
10:6). His face "shone like the sun at its brightest" (Rev 1:16;
cf. Dan 10:6). This sequence of similes conveys the heavenly
glory of this figure. But the significance of the flame-like
eyes may be even more specific. These dazzling, piercing
eyes suggest a Christ able to see beyond external appear-

ances and penetrate the human soul. As he says to the angel of the church in Thyatira, "I am the searcher of hearts and minds" (Rev 2:23).

Perhaps most striking is the description of Christ's voice: "like the sound of rushing water" (literally "like the sound of many waters," Rev 1:15b). This is not straightforward borrowing from Daniel, where the angel's voice was "like the roar of a multitude" (Dan 10:6). Rather, again it emphasizes Christ's divine status. The phrase is derived from Ezekiel's description of the voice of Israel's God, "like the roar of many waters" (Ezek 43:2). This is not the sound of a gentle stream or brook; this is the noise made by a mighty waterfall, like the deafening sound of the Niagara Falls. Christ speaks with a divine voice, powerful and resonant.

STARS, SWORD, AND KEYS

Three further details are noteworthy in this vivid description of Christ: the seven stars in his right hand; the sword protruding from his mouth; and the keys he possesses. Each one adds a further dimension to John's picture of who Christ is and what he has done.

Angels are occasionally symbolized by stars in Jewish tradition (e.g., 1 En 21:3–6). This may reflect the ancient view that the heavenly bodies were living beings, exercising control over human lives. Revelation identifies the seven stars as the angels of the seven congregations, just as it describes the seven golden lampstands as the congregations over which these angels have charge (Rev 1:20). That the angelomorphic Jesus holds them in his right hand vividly conveys his status as higher than the angels and all other cosmic powers.

The description of a sword emerging from the Son of Man's mouth (also Rev 2:12, 16; 19:15) may sound slightly ridiculous. But if one appreciates its biblical background, it can function as a potent symbol. The sword signifies God's word, especially his word of judgment. The mouth of Isaiah's Servant of the Lord is "like a sharp-edged sword" (Isa 49:2). The Book of Wisdom portrays the destroying angel of the exodus as God's Word personified, carrying a sharp sword to carry out God's decree (Wis 18:15). In 4 Ezra, the Messiah destroys the enemies of God's people, not by any traditional weapon of war, but by what issues from his mouth (4 Ezra 13:8–10). Similarly, the risen Christ's only weapon is the word that he speaks. His sword is both sharp and double-edged, an indication that God's word is "sharper than any two-edged sword, penetrating even between soul and spirit, joints and marrow, and able to discern reflections and thoughts of the heart" (Heb 4:12). We may recall Revelation's recurring phrase "the testimony of Jesus." Jesus testifies to the truth, by the powerful, truthful word that he speaks.

Finally, the risen Christ tells John that he holds "the keys to death and the netherworld" (Rev 1:18). The Greek word translated here as "netherworld" is *hadēs*, Hades, the Greek term for Israel's shadowy place of the dead, *Sheol*. In Greek mythology, the keys capable of unlocking the gates of death were held by Hekate, a goddess associated with boundaries. Through the victory of his resurrection, Christ, not Hekate, holds access to the abode of the dead, able to unlock the gates and bring the dead to share his risen life.

THE SWORD-LIKE WORD

He made my mouth like a sharp-edged sword,
concealed me, shielded by his hand.
He made me a sharpened arrow,
in his quiver he hid me. (Isa 49:2)

For when peaceful stillness encompassed everything
and the night in its swift course was half spent,
Your all-powerful word from heaven's royal throne
leapt into the doomed land,
a fierce warrior bearing the sharp sword of your
   inexorable decree,
And alighted, and filled every place with death,
and touched heaven, while standing upon the earth.
(Wis 18:14–16)

When he saw the onrush of the approaching
multitude, he neither lifted his hand nor held a
spear or any weapon of war; but I saw only how he
sent forth from his mouth something like a stream
of fire, and from his lips a flaming breath, and from
his tongue he shot forth a storm of sparks.
(4 Ezra 13:9–10 NRSV)

JOHN'S RESPONSE

A common response to encounters with heavenly beings is fear, prostration, and sometimes collapse. In Daniel, the seer's response to the vision of the man in linen is dramatic: "I fell face forward unconscious" (Dan 10:9). Ezekiel has a similar reaction to "the appearance of the likeness of the glory of the LORD" (Ezek 1:28). Similarly, in Matthew's Gospel, the guards at Christ's tomb are shaken with fear and become like dead men when they see the angel of the Lord (Matt 28:4). There are striking similarities between Revelation's vision of the risen Christ and Matthew's description of this angel: "His appearance was like lightning and his clothing was white as snow" (Matt 28:3).

Human fear is met with reassurance from the heavenly

visitor. The "man dressed in linen" raises Daniel from his prostrate position, telling him not to fear (Dan 10:12). The angel's response to the women at the tomb is "Do not be afraid!" (Matt 28:5). The same pattern is found in Revelation, where John has a similar reaction to the risen Christ: "When I caught sight of him, I fell down at his feet as though dead" (Rev 1:17). Christ then lays his right hand on him, with the reassuring words "Do not be afraid." This is a rhetorically powerful vision, in which the readers or audience share in John's experience of divine encounter.

SUMMARY

John's inaugural vision of "one like a son of man" is evidence that the early Christians found purely human categories (e.g., rabbi, prophet, messiah) insufficient for their growing conviction that Jesus belonged as much to heaven as to the earthly realm. Though he is truly human, and truly died, he appears here as an angelomorphic Christ, a heavenly being. He resembles those exalted angels appearing in human form who manifest God's presence and mediate divine revelation.

But this "one like a son of man" is no mere angel. He holds the angels in his right hand. The hair of his head resembles that of the Ancient of Days. Later, we will discover that the Christ of the Apocalypse, unlike the angels, is worthy of divine worship. Though he is distinct from the one seated on the throne, he participates in the divine glory. This vision holds the human and the divine in dramatic tension. This awesome divine figure may look unfamiliar, but he has a familiar human face: the "eyes like a fiery flame" are the eyes of Jesus of Nazareth. He is the church's great high priest, one of us, close to us, and pleading on our behalf to his heavenly Father. He is the judge, who stands over against the seven churches and exercises judgment over the cosmos.

This vision is rich in OT images, each of which contribute to the whole. But they speak most powerfully by their combined rhetorical effect. Christ's presence is awesome and is meant to take our breath away. This experiential dimension has perhaps been best conveyed by visual artists. In Albrecht Dürer's famous woodcut of the scene, part of his 1498 Apocalypse series, John kneels reverently in prayer before the Son of Man, surrounded by fifteenth-century ecclesiastical candlesticks. The contemporary church participates in John's act of worship. Perhaps even more dramatic is the famous icon by the sixteenth-century Cretan icon writer Thomas Vathas, displayed in the Cave of the Apocalypse on Patmos. John lies prostrate at the bottom of this famous icon, "as if dead." The mysterious Son of Man, surrounded by the seven angels, gazes out at the worshipers, as if inviting them to enter eternity. The only appropriate response is to fall down and worship.

CHAPTER FOUR

The Victorious Lamb

Revelation's preferred title for Christ is one of the best known among Christians: the Lamb. Revelation uses the Greek word *arnion*, a diminutive literally meaning "little sheep" or "little lamb" (John's Gospel uses a different word, *amnos*, for "the Lamb of God," John 1:29, 36). As a christological title, it occurs twenty-eight times throughout the book (it is also used once of the beast from the earth, which "had two horns like a lamb's but spoke like a dragon," Rev 13:11). The number twenty-eight is significant, for it is four times the perfect number seven. Four is the number of the created world. This seems to be a symbolic way of describing the perfect and universal scope of the Lamb's victory.[1]

This chapter will consider the possible background of "the Lamb" as a Jewish title, and explore parallel statements elsewhere in the NT, before examining the key passages where Christ as Lamb appears in the Apocalypse (Rev 4–5; 14:1-5; 21:22-23).

ANIMAL SYMBOLISM

Animal symbolism is common in Jewish and early Christian apocalypses. In symbolic visions, nonhuman

---

1. Richard Bauckham, *The Theology of the Book of Revelation*, New Testament Theology (Cambridge: Cambridge University Press, 1993), 66–67.

animals regularly symbolize humans. One of the most famous is the so-called Animal Apocalypse, comprising chapters 85 — 90 of a composite apocalyptic text called 1 Enoch (chaps. 85 — 90 are generally dated to the second century BCE). It tells the story of humanity, and specifically the people of Israel, from Adam through to the Maccabean revolt and the messianic age. Patriarchs from Adam's son Seth down to Isaac are portrayed as white bulls, Jacob and his descendants as sheep, and Gentile nations as a variety of wild animals, some of which can be identified (e.g., the Egyptians are symbolized as wolves). Sheep as a symbol for God's people picks up on imagery from the prophets (e.g., Ezek 34).

Daniel provides another example of animal symbolism. Daniel 7 describes a terrifying vision of four monstrous beasts, emerging one by one from the sea (vv. 1–8). If ordinary animals symbolize ordinary humans (whether groups or individuals), monsters symbolize oppressive rulers or the kingdoms or empires over which they rule. In the interpretation of Daniel's vision, the reader learns that the beasts represent a succession of kings or empires who have oppressed Israel (7:17, 23): the Babylonians, Medes, Persians, and Greeks. Daniel's vision is an important source for Revelation's vision of the beast from the sea (Rev 13:1–10), an even more monstrous successor to Daniel's four (often thought to symbolize the new empire of Rome).

A third example occurs in 4 Ezra. Ezra receives a vision of a multiwinged, multiheaded eagle rising from the sea and a lion emerging from the forest that denounces the eagle with a human voice and prophesies its downfall (4 Ezra 11). The accompanying interpretation (chap. 12) identifies the eagle as the last beast prophesied in Daniel 7, its heads and feathered wings as specific kings, and the lion as the Messiah. First-century readers would recognize the eagle as a potent symbol of Rome, since the eagle was emblazoned on the standards of Roman legions. Thus 4 Ezra shares with the Apocalypse the conviction that Daniel's vision finds its fuller meaning in the battle between God's people and the forces of imperial Rome. The lion-like features of the Messiah echo Jacob's death-bed blessing of Judah (from whose tribe David, and thus the future royal Messiah, would come) in Genesis (Gen 49:9; cf. 1QSb 5:29).

John's contemporaries, familiar with the Hebrew Scriptures and the apocalyptic tradition, would therefore recognize animal imagery as symbolic of human characters, and monstrous, hybrid creatures, like Daniel's four beasts or 4 Ezra's multiheaded eagle, as symbols of tyrannical rulers or the empires over which they ruled.

LAMB SYMBOLISM

If nonhuman animals symbolize human characters, then Revelation's Lamb symbolizes Christ in his humanity, just as the "one like a son of man" symbolized the exalted, heavenly Christ. But why the Lamb? The answer would appear to lie in John's richly textured interweaving of OT and early Jewish traditions.

Revelation's emphasis on the Lamb's victory might suggest the primary influence of traditions about a warrior lamb. A lamb with a large horn appears in the Animal Apocalypse as a symbol of Judas Maccabeus, leader of the revolt against the Greeks (1 En. 90:9). Similarly, in the Testament of Joseph, the Messiah appears as a destroying lamb or ram (19:8). But other Jewish traditions also seem to be at play. The lamb was a sacrificial animal, a passive victim and therefore a symbol of weakness. A lamb was sacrificed twice a day in the Jerusalem temple, as part of the *tamid* sacrifice

(Exod 29:38–42; Num 28:3–8). Isaiah 53 uses the image to describe the Servant of the Lord, whom the early Christians identified with the suffering Christ, as "like a lamb led to the slaughter or a sheep silent before shearers" (v. 7; cf. Matt 26:63; Acts 8:32).

Most prominent in Revelation, however, is the tradition of the Passover lamb (see also John 1:29; 1 Cor 5:7; 1 Pet 1:18–19). The blood of the Passover lambs marked out the houses of the Israelites in Egypt, sparing their firstborn from death (Exod 12; see Wis 18:14–25), and initiating a chain of events that would lead to the Exodus. As noted in chapter 1, Revelation tells the story of a new exodus in Christ. The redeemed are washed in the blood of the Lamb (Rev 7:14). In the figure of the woman clothed with the sun, understood from earliest times as a symbol of the church, God's people flee into the wilderness, pursued by the great dragon (12:6, 13–14; for the dragon as a symbol of Pharaoh, see Ezek 29:3). Later, we shall encounter the Lamb's people, standing by a sea of glass, singing "the song of Moses, the servant of God, and the song of the Lamb" (Rev 15:3; see Exod 15:1–18). This exodus story provides the primary framework for understanding Christ as the Lamb.

SETTING THE SCENE (REV 4)

The consequence of John's first vision of Christ (Rev 1:9–20) was that John functioned as prophet and scribe, communicating seven messages to seven churches or assemblies of Jesus believers in the Roman province of Asia (the contents of chaps. 2 – 3). At Revelation 4:1, a new section begins. John sees an open door in heaven and is invited to "Come up here." Journeys to heaven, or through multilayered heavens, are frequent features of apocalypses.

The vision of heaven is the key orienting vision of the Apocalypse, to which John will return several times throughout the book (e.g., 7:9–17; 8:2–5; 11:15–18; 15:5–8). At its center stands God's throne, a symbol of power and authority. The recurring message of the book is that the God of Israel is at the center of the cosmos, and that all power and authority derives ultimately from him. But Revelation's heaven is not only a throne room. It is also sacred space, a temple, where every action is directed toward the worship of the one seated on the throne. The one who rules the cosmos is the focus of true worship.

Readers of Revelation 4 should attend to the rhetorical effect of the vision before trying to understand its individual parts. This is a vision meant to evoke God's dazzling glory and the awe-inspiring effects of entering the divine presence. The other details and characters contribute to this overall effect. Four terrifying creatures surround the throne and support it, their many eyes symbolizing their watchfulness as they guard access to God's presence (4:6b–8). John's description draws on Ezekiel's vision of God's throne-chariot supported by four living creatures, the cherubim (Ezek 1:4–14), combined with Isaiah's vision of the Lord's glory in the temple, in which the six-winged seraphim cry out to one another, "Holy, holy, holy is the Lord of hosts! All the earth is filled with his glory!" (Isa 6:3; see Rev 4:8). Each of the four creatures represents one part of the animal world: the lion represents wild animals; the ox or calf, domestic animals; the creature with a human-like face, humanity; and the eagle, the birds (see Midrash Shemoth R. 23). This is a reminder that all creatures, not simply humans, are caught up in the worship of God their Creator.

RABBINIC TRADITION ON THE FOUR LIVING CREATURES OF EZEKIEL 1

> Man is exalted among creatures, the eagle among
> birds, the ox among domestic animals, the lion
> among wild beasts; all of them have received
> dominion....Yet they are stationed below the chariot
> of the Holy One. (Midrash Shemoth R. 23;
> translation from John Sweet, *Revelation*, SCM Pelican
> Commentaries [London: SCM, 1979], 120)

Moving out from the throne, there is a circle of twenty-four elders (Rev 4:4, 10–11), described as both priests (dressed in white, with golden bowls of incense, 5:8) and kings (wearing golden crowns). Whether these are angels or exalted humans, they remind us that Jesus Christ has made God's people "into a kingdom, priests for his God and Father" (1:6). Later, John will describe an even greater outer circle comprising a huge company of angels (literally "myriads of myriads and thousands of thousands," 5:11), also engaged in the worship of the one seated on the throne.

Though both Ezekiel and Isaiah have influenced John's description, his is no mere literary borrowing. There is evidence that Jewish mystics meditated on certain scriptural passages, including the first chapter of Ezekiel, as preparation for their own visionary experience. Certainly, these important prophetic visions provide the raw material for what John describes. But there is a dynamism to John's account, as well as details unique to him (e.g., the twenty-four elders), that suggest genuine visionary experience underlying what he writes.

Nor are Israel's Scriptures the only influence on Revelation 4. John's first audiences would also have recognized similarities between this heavenly throne room and the emperor's throne room in Rome. It raises the question sharply: Where is true power to be found? In Rome's military might? Or in the alternative space of heaven into which John has entered? Surprisingly, whereas the gods of Rome, and the deified emperors, are visualized in human form, John steadfastly avoids anthropomorphic descriptions of the one seated on the throne. Instead, he relies on images from the mineral world, evoking the awesome, dazzling presence of the deity: "A throne was there in heaven, and on the throne sat one whose appearance sparkled like jasper and carnelian. Around the throne was a halo as brilliant as an emerald" (Rev 4:2b–3). The enthroned emperor, or the human-like gods of Rome, are as nothing compared with the glorious God of Israel, who alone governs the cosmos.

THE LION AND THE LAMB (REV 5)

It is within this vision of God's heavenly glory that the Lamb makes his first appearance. John sees in the right hand of the one on the throne a scroll with writing on back and front, sealed with seven seals (Rev 5:1). Scholars are divided as to precisely what this scroll contains: proposals include the OT, specific prophetic passages, or the contents of John's visions in the remainder of the book. Whatever the specific contents, it seems clear that this scroll contains God's plan to put the world right, overcoming all that stands in the way (evil, injustice, the oppression of beastly empires) of his will for creation. But it can only be put into effect when all seven seals are broken, and the scroll fully opened. Hence John's emotional reaction when he hears that no one is worthy to open the scroll: "I shed many tears because no one was found worthy to open the scroll or to examine it" (5:4).

The story now takes a dramatic turn, as one of the twenty-four elders reassures John that "the lion of the tribe of Judah, the root of David, has triumphed, enabling him to open the scroll with its seven seals" (5:5). Lions in the biblical world, as in other cultures, were symbols of power (e.g., Prov 30:30; Ps 17:12). But the lion reference here is more specific. As in 4 Ezra's aforementioned vision of the lion-Messiah (4 Ezra 11:37–46; 12:31–34), this passage recalls Jacob's blessing of Judah in Genesis 49:9. The lion of the tribe of Judah is the end-time Messiah or anointed king of David's line. The accompanying phrase "the root of David" recalls Isaiah's prophecy about a shoot from the stump of Jesse, David's father, which similarly looks forward to the restoration of the Davidic monarchy (Isa 11:1; cf. Jer 23:5). The reader of Revelation is led to expect the appearance of the victorious lion-like Messiah.

OT BACKGROUND TO REV 5:5

> Judah is a lion's cub,
> you have grown up on prey, my son.
> He crouches, lies down like a lion,
> like a lioness—who would dare rouse him?
> The scepter shall never depart from Judah,
> or the mace from between his feet,
> Until tribute comes to him,
> and he receives the people's obedience. (Gen 49:9–10)

> But a shoot shall sprout from the stump of Jesse,
> and from his roots a bud shall blossom.
> The spirit of the LORD shall rest upon him:
> a spirit of wisdom and of understanding,

A spirit of counsel and of strength,
a spirit of knowledge and of fear of the LORD,
and his delight shall be the fear of the LORD. (Isa
    11:1–3a)

See, days are coming—oracle of the LORD—
when I will raise up a righteous branch for David;
As king he shall reign and govern wisely,
he shall do what is just and right in the land. (Jer 23:5)

Instead, John sees a sacrificial victim. An expected image of leonine power is apparently thwarted by an image of weakness. For some scholars, the lion is totally redefined by the Lamb. Yet rather than allowing the lion image to be completely subsumed by the Lamb symbol, we should allow the two to mutually interpret each other. The Lamb that John sees is lion-like, but what it means to be a lion is redefined by attending to aspects of the Lamb. As the African American NT scholar Brian Blount expresses this paradox, the Lamb "conquers by predatory weakness."[2]

JOHN'S DESCRIPTION OF THE LAMB

Three aspects of John's description of Christ as the Lamb (Rev 5:6–10) merit specific comment. First, although this Lamb "seemed to have been slain," it is standing. This is a vivid example of how apocalyptic visions stretch the boundaries of our imaginations, for slaughtered animals do

---

2. Brian K. Blount, *Can I Get a Witness? Reading Revelation through African American Culture* (Louisville, KY: Westminster John Knox, 2005), 86.

not normally stand! One may recall Umberto Eco's definition of an apocalypse cited earlier: "the vision of the outsider, or of the artist who makes us see by making things strange." What the Apocalypse "makes us see" is that, despite appearances to the contrary, the sacrificial slaughter of the Lamb is a victorious death. Christ has conquered, not by slaughtering his enemies as the Messiah might be expected to, but by submitting to death himself. When John sees the slaughtered yet standing Lamb in heaven, he sees in visionary form the victory of the cross: Christ vindicated, raised, and exalted to heaven, bringing with him the now-glorious wounds of his passion. What looks like weakness and defeat is "unveiled" (the root meaning of "apocalypse") as a powerful victory.

Two further aspects of John's description underscore this point. The Lamb has seven horns and seven eyes (5:6b). Taken literally, this would be a grotesque animal. Yet again, we find ourselves in the fantastical world of apocalyptic images. The number seven symbolizes perfection or completion. In the Bible, a "horn" is a symbol of power (e.g., 1 Sam 2:1; Ps 18:2; Luke 1:69). The Lamb's seven horns therefore signify that the crucified and risen Christ is all-powerful. Similarly, the Lamb's seven eyes symbolize Christ's omniscience. He is all-seeing, and all-knowing.

OTHER REFERENCE TO THE LAMB IN REVELATION

The Lamb will continue as major actor in the remainder of the book. Indeed, this first visionary appearance continues into Revelation 6, where the Lamb, having received the scroll from the one seated on the throne, now opens its seals one by one, thus orchestrating the events John describes: the appearance of the four horsemen, iconic symbols of victory, war, famine, and death (6:1–8); the vision of the martyrs under the heavenly altar, crying out for God to act against their persecutors (6:9–11); the description of the last day (6:12–17) in which humans seek to hide from "the face of the one who sits on the throne and from the wrath of the Lamb" (6:16). The Lamb thereby functions as agent of the one on the throne, instrumental in the chain of events whereby the forces of evil and chaos are defeated and God's salvation is established.

The Lamb reappears in the next chapter, in which John receives a vision of salvation, after the tribulations of the end (7:9–17). This vision of a huge gathering of nations and languages presents an expanded people of God. They wear white robes, like the slaughtered martyrs under the altar at 6:11, and have palm branches, symbols of victory, in their hands. These also seem to be martyrs, or at least those willing to lay down their lives for the faith, having come through "the time of great distress" (7:14, the "messianic woes" that many Jews expected would precede the coming of the end). In one of Revelation's paradoxes, they are said to have "washed their robes and made them white" in the Lamb's blood (7:14; see also 12:11). John is also told that the Lamb "will shepherd them and lead them to springs of life-giving water" (7:17). Here is another paradox: Christ is both Lamb and Shepherd of the flock (a similar claim is made by John's Gospel: 1:29, 36; 10:11–18).

Another vision in which the Lamb plays a central role is described at Revelation 14:1–5. Here John sees the Lamb standing on Mount Zion, that is, Jerusalem (though it is unclear whether he means the earthly or the heavenly city). Mount Zion was often used as shorthand for the Temple Mount, the place of God's presence. The Lamb is accompanied by the 144,000, his army of victorious witnesses or martyrs (see 7:1–8).

Finally, the Lamb reappears in the climactic vision of ultimate salvation, the New Jerusalem (21:9 — 22:5). Not only does this vision contain a reference to "the twelve apostles of the Lamb," whose names are inscribed on the foundations of the holy city (21:14; cf. Eph 2:19–20). John tells us that God and the Lamb will dwell within the city, making any additional temple unnecessary. Again, the close relationship between God and the Lamb is emphasized: the Lamb is the lamp that radiates the light of God's glory (Rev 21:23); judgment occurs according to what is written in "the Lamb's book of life" (21:27; cf. 13:8); God and the Lamb share a single throne, and both are the objects of worship (22:1, 3).

In addition to these "on-stage" appearances of the Lamb as character in the drama, there are passing references to this character that contribute to the audience's overall understanding. We hear, for example, that the Lamb is involved in a war with the beast's ten horns, symbolizing ten kings, but that "the Lamb will conquer them, for he is Lord of lords and king of kings" (17:14). At Revelation 15:3, those who have gained victory over the beast sing "the song of Moses, the servant of God, and the song of the Lamb." The story of the exodus is here evoked, thus highlighting Christ's role as the new Passover Lamb, who liberates his people from sin and death. Finally, after the fall of the great city Babylon, the Lamb's wedding day is announced and those invited to the wedding feast are pronounced blessed (19:7, 9). As in the Gospel of John, Christ is presented here as the bridegroom of his people (John 2:1–12; 3:29). These multiple references to the Lamb in nine separate chapters of Revelation underscore its importance as the book's guiding christological title.

SUMMARY

If the vision of the exalted Christ in Revelation 1:12–20 emphasized Christ's divinity, the vision of the slaughtered Lamb emphasizes his humanity. Building on the apocalyptic tradition of animal symbolism to denote humans, and lion and lamb figures to signify messianic figures, the Apocalypse offers a symbolic portrayal of Christ's human self-sacrifice. Christ as the slaughtered-yet-standing Lamb conquers through dying, through becoming the powerless victim. His power is made known in weakness. As the new Passover Lamb, he leads his new people from slavery to freedom. The story of the Lamb is nothing less than the victory of the cross: "Christ has died; Christ is risen; Christ will come again."

Christ as the victorious Lamb has been an influential image in Christian art across the centuries, found already on early Christian sarcophagi and in the mosaics decorating the ancient basilicas of Rome and Ravenna. The artistic tradition has had to confront the problem raised by the text: Should one emphasize the power of this symbol (the fact that it is "standing," and has "seven horns"), or its weakness ("slaughtered")? Or is there a way of conveying both dimensions simultaneously? The Lamb in the sixth-century apse mosaic of San Vitale in Ravenna is very much alive. It stands robustly, surrounded by a victory wreath and supported by angels, with no indication of its sacrificial death. By contrast, the Lamb in William Blake's *Four and Twenty Elders Casting Their Crowns before the Divine Throne* (ca. 1803–5; Tate Britain, London) is almost invisible, lying motionless at the feet of God's throne. Almost incidental to the scene, Blake's Lamb is an evocative image of weakness and vulnerability. The famous *Ghent Altarpiece* by Hubert and Jan van Eyck (ca. 1432) combines both aspects. The Lamb stands on an altar in the central panel, gazing directly out at the viewer, its blood poured out into a chalice.[3]

The Ghent Lamb highlights the connection between this key christological title and the Christian Eucharist, a participation in "the wedding feast of the Lamb" (Rev 19:9). Another is the presence of the seven-horned, seven-eyed Lamb over the main altar in the Basilica of the National Shrine of the Immaculate Conception, in Washington, D.C. In the Mass, eternity breaks into the present. The worship of the earthly church, where in Washington or Rome or the first-century house-churches of Pergamum or Thyatira, is caught up into the worship of heaven:

> Worthy is the Lamb that was slain
>> to receive power and riches, wisdom and
>> strength,
> honor and glory and blessing. (Rev 5:12)

---

3. For a fuller discussion of the Lamb in visual art and music, see Natasha O'Hear and Anthony O'Hear, *Picturing the Apocalypse: The Book of Revelation in the Arts over Two Millennia* (Oxford: Oxford University Press, 2015), 52–69.

CHAPTER FIVE

The Peaceable Warrior

Many Christian readers, particularly in the modern world, are offended by the violence of the Book of Revelation, and the militaristic language used to describe both Jesus and his people. One aspect of the Lamb's role is that of military leader and victor, echoing the warrior lamb or ram of the Animal Apocalypse and the Testament of Joseph. The Lamb wages war (e.g., Rev 17:14) and has armies who wage war with him (e.g., 12:11; 14:1). Moreover, there are several battle scenes throughout the book, particularly in the last few chapters, which describe the climax of history and the final victory of God's plan (16:16; 19:17–21; 20:7–10). In addition, we hear of humans seeking to escape from "the face of the one who sits on the throne and from the wrath of the Lamb" (6:16b) and read of a disturbing scene that apparently gloats over the eternal torment of worshipers of the beast in the Lamb's presence (14:9–10).

Such military images, and the presence of passages describing violence and bloodshed, seem hard to reconcile with a Christian vision of the Prince of Peace, whose birth was announced as bringing peace on earth (Luke 2:14), who eschewed violence at his arrest (Matt 26:52–54), and was himself the victim of a violent death at the hands of others. But it is perhaps Revelation's vision of the rider on the white horse that, to many Christian readers, is the most surprising, and even shocking, depiction of Jesus in the whole Book of Revelation (19:11–16). John sees heaven opened (as he had before, e.g., 4:1; 11:19), a crucial moment of divine "unveiling" or "apocalypse." In the Gospels, the heavens were "opened" at Jesus's baptism, revealing him to be the Son of God (Matt 3:16; Luke 3:21; Mark 1:10 has "torn open"). In John's vision, a terrifying warrior figure emerges who is identified as "the Word of God" (Rev 19:13). He rides a white horse, probably a war horse, and has a sword protruding from his mouth. John tells us that this rider "will tread out in the wine press the wine of the fury and wrath of God the almighty" (19:15). This stands in sharp contrast to the evangelists' description of Christ's entry into Jerusalem, where his unpretentious donkey replaces the war horses typically ridden by conquering heroes (Matt 21:1–9; Mark 11:1–10; Luke 19:28–40).

This chapter will examine this potent vision, one of the main biblical sources for the "Battle Hymn of the Republic," to explore how the Apocalypse reworks traditions about the Divine Warrior to interpret Christ's victory. It begins with a brief discussion of Revelation 12, which helps prepare the ground for the vision of the rider in 19:11–21. It will then consider the relationship of this rider to a previous character who also rides a white horse (6:2). The bulk of this chapter will examine the details of the Divine Warrior vision, reflecting on what this contributes to Revelation's overall portrait of Jesus Christ.

BATTLE HYMN OF THE REPUBLIC

> Mine eyes have seen the glory of the coming of the Lord:
> He is trampling out the vintage where the grapes of
>   wrath are stored;
> He hath loosed the fateful lightning of His terrible swift
>   sword:

His truth is marching on. (Julia Ward Howe, 1861; in
the public domain)

PREPARING THE GROUND: THE MALE CHILD OF REVELATION 12

As discussed in chapter 1, Revelation 12 seems to mark a new beginning in the story. The blowing of the seventh trumpet announced the arrival of God's kingdom (11:15–18). Yet with the opening of the heavenly temple at 11:19, the story begins all over again. The confrontation between a woman and a serpent recalls Eve in the Garden of Eden. The twelve stars on the woman's crown (a symbol of Israel's twelve tribes, Gen 37:9–11) suggests that this woman's story is primarily the story of Israel, the people from whom the Messiah was born. For much of Christian history, well into the Middle Ages, this woman clothed with the sun was interpreted as an image of God's people, or specifically the church. This may surprise many Catholics, who understand the woman to be Mary, reflected liturgically in the reading of this passage at Mass on the Solemnity of the Assumption of Our Lady (August 15). The Marian interpretation is a secondary interpretation, developing out of the conviction that Mary is an image of the church (see, e.g., Vatican II, *Lumen Gentium* 60–65).

But our focus here is less on the woman (whether Eve, Israel, Jerusalem, Mary, or the church), but on her son. Revelation 12 describes the Messiah, the longed-for hope of God's people, as "a son, a male child, destined to rule all the nations with an iron rod" (12:5a). This description draws on Psalm 2, also used by John at Revelation 2:26–27 (there of Christ's victorious people who share in his royal rule), 11:15–18, and 14:1–5. It will be reprised in the vision of the Divine Warrior at 19:11–16. Psalm 2, possibly composed for a royal coronation in Jerusalem, is read here as a prophecy of the royal Messiah, acclaimed by God as "my son" (Ps 2:7).

Three points may be made about the woman's male child. First, he is a royal, military figure, who will "rule all the nations" (Ps 2 speaks of God's anointed king thwarting the foreign kings who plot against him). The story of the woman and her child is interwoven with the heavenly battle between the armies of Michael and the armies of Satan, in which the victory is achieved not primarily by the angelic forces but "by the blood of the Lamb" and the testimony of the martyrs (Rev 12:10–12). The male child has his own soldiers.

Second, however, the reference to "the blood of the Lamb" and the martyrs reminds us that the male warrior is engaged in no ordinary war. He will conquer by being killed. This might explain the peculiar fact that the child is "caught up to God and his throne" immediately after birth (12:5b). The "birth" may be less a literal reference to Christ's birth at Bethlehem than to his death and resurrection, followed by his ascension to God's right hand (Acts 2:33; 13:33; Rom 1:4; Heb 1:3). This fleshes out Revelation's previous description of Christ as "the firstborn of the dead" (Rev 1:5). Nor is his subsequent rule over the nations necessarily one of authoritarian domination. The verb translated "rule" can also mean "shepherd," an appropriate description for Christ the Lamb who is also a shepherd (7:17).

The third point would be of specific relevance to John's first audiences, living in the Roman province of Asia. Revelation 12 has strong echoes of the myth of the birth of the god Apollo, whose pregnant mother, Leto, was threatened by Python, a giant serpent. Apollo would later kill Python, thus bringing order out of chaos. These echoes of the Apollo myth are all the more striking when one recalls that John's island of Patmos was dedicated to Apollo's twin sister, Artemis, that Ephesus had a famous temple to Artemis, and that one of the most important shrines of Apollo was located approximately fifty miles south of Ephesus, at Didyma. For Revelation, it is not Apollo but Jesus Christ who has defeated the dragon-serpent, bringing order out of chaos.

TWO RIDERS ON WHITE HORSES (REV 19:11 AND 6:2)

The victorious male child of Revelation prepares the ground for the vision of the rider on the white horse, who is also said to rule the nations "with an iron rod" (Rev 19:15; cf. Ps 2:9). But one further issue needs to be resolved before we proceed. What is the relationship between this rider and the first of the Apocalypse's four horsemen (Rev 6:1–8), who also rides a white horse? John writes of this rider, "I looked, and there was a white horse, and its rider had a bow. He was given a crown, and he rode forth victorious to further his victories" (6:2). Many commentators from the second century onward have also interpreted this horseman as Christ, riding out to victory as he proclaims the gospel (e.g., Irenaeus, *Adv. Haer.* 4.21.3). This interpretation is regularly found in Christian art. A modern example is the dramatic mural by Jan Henryk de Rosen (1943), located in the headquarters of the United States Conference of Catholic Bishops in Washington, D.C. Here the first rider of Revelation 6:2 is clearly Christ, since he dwarfs the three remaining horsemen and turns his bow on them.

This positive interpretation is understandable. The emergence of the four horsemen follows immediately from the exalted Lamb opening the first seals of the scroll given him by God. There is, in other words, an intimate connection between the victory of the crucified and risen Christ and the appearance of the first rider. Moreover, white symbolizes victory throughout the book. However, the Lamb and the rider appear to be different characters. Thus, one finds some variation in early Christian interpretations of Revelation 6:2, identifying the Lamb and the horseman as distinct, though closely related. According to the earliest surviving Latin commentary on the Apocalypse by Victorinus of Pettau (third century), this rider symbolizes the Holy Spirit, sent by the Son following his ascension. Alternatively, the first rider is an image of the gospel, achieving victory as it is preached throughout the world (e.g., the sixth-century Greek commentary of Andrew of Caesarea).

Still other commentators drive a sharper wedge between the rider of 19:11–16 and the rider on the white horse of 6:2. They note that, despite their superficial similarities, there are also striking differences. For example, the first rider's weapon is a bow. John's original audiences may have detected a reference to Rome's enemies, the Parthians, whose calvary carried bows. By contrast, the Divine Warrior wields only the sword coming from his mouth (19:15; see 1:16).

According to this interpretation, the first rider of Revelation 6:2 is a pseudo-Christ, an antichrist figure. The Apocalypse contains several figures who deceive through a superficial resemblance to characters on the side of God. The dragon has seven heads, a number symbolizing perfection (12:3). The first beast similarly has seven heads but is revealed as a terrifying monster (13:1–2). The second beast that emerges "out of the earth" or "from the land" has two lamb's horns. Yet, despite its similarities to Christ the Lamb, its demonic origins are betrayed by the fact that it "spoke like a dragon" (13:11). Many scholars have seen a connection between Revelation 6 and Jesus's final sermon in the Synoptic Gospels (often referred to as the "Eschatological Discourse" or the "Little Apocalypse"). In that sermon, Christ warns his disciples against "false messiahs" who will deceive many (Matt 24:5, 24; Mark 13:6, 22; Luke 21:8). Perhaps Revelation's first rider is also an antichrist figure, one of those destructive forces (along with his companions, war, famine, and death) that, paradoxically, now fall under the Lamb's control. Out of destruction and chaos, the Lamb is building a new world.

Whichever interpretation of Revelation 6:2 is offered, the rider of chapter 19 is clearly Christ himself, coming in judgment. The remainder of this chapter will examine this vision, its background in the Divine Warrior tradition, and its contribution to the Christology of Revelation.

CHRIST AS DIVINE WARRIOR

This vision of Christ occurs as part of a series of seven visions (Rev 19:11 – 21:8) describing the final victory of Christ and defeat of "those who destroy the earth" (11:18): the beast and false prophet; the dragon/Satan; Death and Hades. John describes this vision thus:

> Then I saw the heavens opened, and there was a white horse; its rider was [called] "Faithful and True." He judges and wages war in righteousness. His eyes were [like] a fiery flame, and on his head were many diadems. He had a name inscribed that no one knows except himself. He wore a cloak that had been dipped in blood, and his name was called the Word of God. The armies of

heaven followed him, mounted on white horses and wearing clean white linen. Out of his mouth came a sharp sword to strike the nations. He will rule them with an iron rod, and he himself will tread out in the wine press the wine of the fury and wrath of God the almighty. He has a name written on his cloak and on his thigh, "King of kings and Lord of lords." (19:11–16)

SEVEN FINAL VISIONS

1. The Rider on the White Horse (19:11–16)
2. The Victory over the Beast and the False Prophet (19:17–21)
3. The Binding of Satan (20:1–3)
4. The Millennial Reign of the Martyrs with Christ (20:4–6)
5. The Release of Satan (20:7–10)
6. The Last Judgment (20:11–15)
7. The New Heavens and the New Earth (21:1–8)

John's disturbing vision taps into an ancient tradition of the Divine Warrior, widespread in the ancient Near East and finding expression in various OT passages. Using language drawn from human life, God is often described as a warrior who defends the people of Israel from their enemies, fighting on their behalf. In some later Jewish texts, such as the Psalms of Solomon (first century BCE) or 2 Baruch (late first century CE), the Divine Warrior role is transferred to the Messiah (Pss. Sol. 17; 2 Bar 72). Perhaps closest to Revelation 19 is the vision of YHWH as Divine Warrior in Isaiah 63. The prophet sees the Lord return from Bozrah, a city of Edom, having defeated the Edomites in battle. His crimsoned clothes are drenched with the blood of Israel's enemies; his treading the wine press is a symbol of judgment.

Jewish exegesis would eventually combine Isaiah's vision with the blessing of Judah in Genesis 49, thus identifying the terrifying Divine Warrior as the royal Messiah. Such a reading occurs in the Palestinian Targum (an Aramaic translation/paraphrase of the Hebrew Bible for Aramaic-speaking Jews) on Genesis. John may be aware of a similar exegetical tradition in presenting Jesus as a warrior Messiah, in a vision that repeats key elements of Isaiah 63 (clothing dipped in blood; the treading of the wine press).

THE DIVINE WARRIOR

> Who is this that comes from Edom,
> in crimsoned garments, from Bozrah?
> Who is this, glorious in his apparel,
> striding in the greatness of his strength?
> "It is I, I who announce vindication,
> mighty to save."
> Why is your apparel red,
> and your garments like one who treads the wine press?
> "The wine press I have trodden alone,
> and from the peoples no one was with me.
> I trod them in my anger,
> and trampled them down in my wrath;
> Their blood spurted on my garments,
> all my apparel I stained." (Isa 63:1-3)

> In wisdom, in righteousness, may he expel sinners from
> the inheritance:
> May he smash the sinner's arrogance like a potter's
> vessel.

With a rod of iron may he break in pieces all their
substance:
May he destroy the lawless nations by the word of his
mouth. (Pss. Sol. 17:23–27; trans. S. P. Brock in
Sparks)

After the signs have appeared, which you were told
about before, when the nations are in confusion,
and the time of my Messiah is come, he will call all
the nations together, and some of them he will
spare, and some of them he will destroy....But all
those who have had dominion over you, or have
exploited you, will be given over to the sword.
(2 Bar. 72:2, 6; trans. R. H. Charles and L. H.
Brockington in Sparks)

How beautiful is the King Messiah who is to arise
from among those of the house of Judah! He girds
his loins and goes out to wage war on those who
hate him, and slays kings with their rulers, making
the mountains red with the blood of their slain and
making the hills white with the fat of their warriors
and his vestments are soaked in blood. He is like the
presser of grapes. (Palestinian Targum on Genesis
49:11)[1]

Yet in John's apocalyptic reimagining, things are not
always what they seem. Three features of this vision suggest that John presents a dramatic "rebirth of images"[2] as

---

1. Translation from Martin McNamara, *The New Testament and the Palestinian Targum to the Pentateuch*, Analecta Biblica 27 (Rome: Pontifical Biblical Institute, 1966), 232.

2. The phrase comes from the English NT scholar Austin Farrer. Austin Farrer, *A Rebirth of Images: The Making of John's Apocalypse* (Westminster: Dacre Press, 1949).

the traditional Divine Warrior myth is placed at the service of the gospel story of Christ's victory through suffering, death, and resurrection. The first relates to the rider's clothing. When John glimpses him in the open heavens, he wears a robe "that had been dipped in blood" (Rev 19:13). Yet in contrast to the "crimsoned garments" in Isaiah, the robe is bloodied before the battle has been engaged. For many commentators, this is not the blood of Christ's enemies, but his own blood, which has been mentioned multiple times already (1:5; 5:9; 7:14; 12:11). As Origen (ca. 184–ca. 253), the great biblical scholar of the early church, put it: "He is clothed with a garment sprinkled with blood, since the Word who became flesh, and died because he became flesh, is invested with traces of that passion, since his blood also was poured forth upon the earth when the soldier pierced his side."[3]

The second striking feature pertains to Christ's weapon. Warriors need effective weapons to win a war. Yet Christ does not wield his weapon — his sharp sword — in his hand. Rather, it emerges from his mouth. As discussed in chapter 3, this is no literal weapon, but Christ's challenging, saving, and destructive word. This is a battle of words, of truth versus falsehood.

The third hint of a dramatic "rebirth of images" relates to the Divine Warrior's accompanying armies, "mounted on white horses and wearing clean white linen" (19:14). Early Christian tradition expected Christ to return in glory accompanied by the holy angels (e.g., Matt 16:27; 25:31; Mark 8:38; 2 Thess 1:7). Angels are sometimes portrayed dressed in white (e.g., Matt 28:3; Mark 16:5; John 20:12) or wearing linen (e.g., Dan 10:5; 12:6–7). One might reasonably conclude, therefore, that Christ's calvary are the angelic

---

3. Origen, *Commentary on the Gospel of John: Books 1–10*, trans. R. C. Heine, FC 80 (Washington, DC: Catholic University of America Press, 1989), 110.

hosts. Yet hints from earlier in the Apocalypse suggest an alternative: that this heavenly army comprises the victorious martyrs, or the larger body of Christ's people. These have "washed their robes and made them white in the blood of the Lamb" (Rev 7:14; see also 3:5). Moreover, John has just been told that the Lamb's Bride wore "a bright, clean linen garment," which "represents the righteous deeds of the holy ones" (19:8). The military prowess of this rider is supported, not so much by sword-wielding angels, but an army of faithful followers who have followed the Lamb's way of sacrifice.

NAMES OF CHRIST

Further insight into Christ the Divine Warrior is provided by the succession of titles and names ascribed to him. Four are mentioned: "Faithful and True" (19:11); a name "that no one knows except himself" (19:12); the "Word of God" (19:13); "King of kings and Lord of lords" (19:16). We shall consider each in turn, though reserving discussion of the mysterious unknown name until last.

First, the rider is called "Faithful and True" (19:11). Christ has previously been introduced as the "faithful witness" (1:5), expanded to "the faithful and true witness" in the message to the angel of the church in Laodicea (3:14). This underscores Jesus's fidelity and reliability ("reliable" or "trustworthy" are other possible translations of the Greek *pistos*, "faithful," while *alēthinos*, "true," can also mean "dependable" or "genuine"). This faithfulness and truthfulness are also demanded of Jesus's followers (one of his own martyrs, Antipas of Pergamum, was similarly described as "my faithful witness," 2:13). This sets Christ and his people in sharp contrast to the dragon and his unreliable beasts, who deceive humanity (e.g., 12:9; 13:14).

Second, "his name was called the Word of God" (19:13). This is one of several points at which, for all their differences in style and vocabulary, the Apocalypse and the Fourth Gospel coincide. In the Gospel of John, the term is used absolutely, without the qualifier "of God," to describe the preexistent Word or Logos, active in creation and in ongoing revelation to humanity, and especially Israel, throughout salvation history. This life-giving, revealing Word has now become incarnate, made flesh, in the human Jesus of Nazareth (John 1:1–18). By contrast, Revelation focuses on the war-like word of God. Like the sword emerging from the warrior's mouth, God's word challenges and convicts, cutting keenly (see Heb 4:12). The image John presents here is reminiscent of the following passage from the Book of Wisdom, probably written in Alexandria, Egypt, in the first century BCE:

> For when peaceful stillness encompassed
> everything
> and the night in its swift course was half
> spent,
> Your all-powerful word from heaven's royal
> throne
> leapt into the doomed land,
> a fierce warrior bearing the sharp sword of your
> inexorable decree,
> And alighted, and filled every place with death,
> and touched heaven, while standing upon the
> earth. (Wis 18:14–16)

The author of Wisdom is retelling the story of the first Passover and exodus. God's "all-powerful word" here is the angel of death, and "the doomed land," the land of Egypt. John too views the Word of God as a warrior, wielding a sharp sword. The imagery, however, is transformed by the story of Christ's cross.

A third title is written "on his cloak and on his thigh": "King of kings and Lord of lords" (Rev 19:16; see 17:14). As we saw in chapter 2, a similar title was used of God in the Greek version of Daniel ("Lord of lords and King of kings," Dan 4:37 LXX). This title speaks of Christ's royal authority, underscored by the fact that he has "many diadems" on his head (Rev 19:12). This number contrasts with the more limited authority of the dragon (seven diadems, 12:3) and the beast (ten, 13:1). In addition, there may be an allusion to Christ's high priestly role, for Aaron wore a crown or diadem (Wis 18:24).

Most mysterious is that fourth name: "a name inscribed that no one knows except himself" (Rev 19:12; see 3:12: "my new name"). This may reflect the ancient conviction that names reveal a person's character, and to know someone's name is to gain control over them. That Christ has an unknown name therefore preserves his sovereign authority. However, some scholars think that this "unknown name" is the tetragrammaton, YHWH, the unpronounceable name of God. Strictly speaking, YHWH is not a name but the statement of a mystery: "I am who I am" (Exod 3:14). The notion that Christ shares God's name is not unique to Revelation. In the Gospel of John, Jesus speaks of having come in his Father's name (5:43) or revealing his Father's name (17:6, 26). In the Philippians hymn, Jesus is said to inherit "the name that is above every name" (Phil 2:9). In sharing God's name, Jesus shares God's character, and is invested with God's authority.

SUMMARY

John's vision of the rider on a white horse further builds on, and complements, the various images of Jesus that have gradually unfolded, chapter by chapter, throughout the Apocalypse. To see Christ as a terrifying warrior, riding out in judgment with his army, may be unfamiliar to many (though it is present in hymns such as the "Battle Hymn of the Republic" or "Onward, Christian Soldiers"). But this image makes a crucial contribution to the overall picture of Revelation's Christ. The language of warfare reminds us that there is a real battle at the heart of the cosmos, between good and evil, light and darkness. The modern world, which has seen two world wars, multiple genocides, and the cruel regimes of many dictators, knows this to be true. Like the Gospel of John, which reveals God's Word as a light that the darkness has not overcome (John 1:5), the Apocalypse presents this cosmic conflict in dramatic symbolic language.

However, the image of Christ the Divine Warrior also reassures us that this battle has been definitively won, though in a manner that turns the standards of human warfare on its head. Christ has conquered by allowing himself to be killed. The Lamb shows his saving power in weakness. Christ the Divine Warrior has no weapon in his hand; his sword is the word of truth, the word that he embodies as the Word of God, who is "Faithful and True." His accompanying army comprises those who have taken the way of the Lamb to heart, conquering through speaking the truth at the risk of dying for it (see Rev 12:11). Again, we have a visionary description of the victory of the cross.

Taking seriously the "rebirth of images" helps ameliorate some of the militaristic, even violent dimensions of this vision, which for many Christians are difficult to reconcile with a Jesus who refuses to rely on angelic support when he is arrested (Matt 26:53–54), teaches his followers to turn the other cheek (Matt 5:39; Luke 6:29), and warns his disciples that "all who take the sword will perish by the sword" (Matt 26:52). There is a violence to the gospel of Christ, in its battle with evil, falsehood, and injustice. However, in the words of St. Óscar Romero, himself a martyred follower of the Lamb, it is "the violence of love."

CHAPTER SIX

The Worship of Christ in Revelation

The first audiences of John's Apocalypse almost certainly heard the book when they were gathered for worship. These small congregations of believers, meeting in private homes or hired halls, would have represented a tiny percentage of their cities' populations. One scholarly estimate puts the Christian community in Ephesus at between fifty and a hundred believers, out of a total population of perhaps two hundred thousand.[1] Members of the seven churches would have been surrounded by buildings dedicated to worship: temples where sacrifice was offered to the gods, or where deified emperors were worshiped. Those from a Jewish background would also retain a memory of the temple in Jerusalem, the locus of God's presence among his people. Their own gatherings for worship would have felt quite different. Yet as the story of Revelation was read aloud to them, they would have been caught up into the heavenly, angelic liturgy it describes. God's throne room in the Apocalypse is also the heavenly temple, on which the earthly sanctuary was believed to have been modelled.

Central to this early Christian experience of worship was the risen Jesus, experienced among them as a life-giving

---

1. Wes Howard-Brook and Anthony Gwyther, *Unveiling Empire: Reading Revelation Then and Now* (Maryknoll, NY: Orbis, 1999), xxii.

presence. We saw this exemplified in Revelation's opening vision, where the one like a son of man stands in the midst of the seven churches, as their glorious high priest. This chapter will explore how the Apocalypse presents Christ as sharing in the honor due to God alone, a striking motif given the book's strictures against false worship. It will reprise some of the titles of Christ discussed in chapter 2, as well as the canticles addressed to the Lamb, to explore the close relationship between Christ and God throughout the book. All this contributes to what some NT scholars have considered one of the highest Christologies in the whole NT.

TRUE AND FALSE WORSHIP

The Apocalypse is dominated by the theme of worship. There is false worship (idolatry), which makes the fundamental error of investing ultimate honor in that which cannot save or satisfy. This is exemplified in the worship of the dragon (Rev 13:4), the worship of the beast from the sea and its cult image (13:4, 8, 12, 15; 14:9, 11; 16:2; 19:20; 20:4), and the worship of demons and idols (9:20). Yet this stricture against false worship is not confined to evil characters. It also extends to the angelic realm. On two occasions, John attempts to worship his accompanying angel, only to be firmly rebuked: "Worship God" (19:10; 22:9). The angel is not the source of the revelation he brings but only its messenger. In this, he is simply a "fellow servant" of John and other early Christian prophets, who also communicate God's word. A similar scene occurs in the early Christian apocalypse known as the Ascension of Isaiah (probably second century CE), which traces Isaiah's journey up to the seventh heaven. Isaiah attempts to worship an enthroned figure he sees in the second heaven, but is forbidden from doing so by his angelic companion (Ascen. Isa. 7:21–22).

COMMANDS AGAINST WORSHIPING ANGELS

"I fell at his feet to worship him. But he said to me, 'Don't! I am a fellow servant of yours and of your brothers who bear witness to Jesus. Worship God. Witness to Jesus is the spirit of prophecy'" (Rev 19:10).

"It is I, John, who heard and saw these things, and when I heard and saw them I fell down to worship at the feet of the angel who showed them to me. But he said to me, 'Don't! I am a fellow servant of yours and of your brothers the prophets and of those who keep the message of this book. Worship God'" (Rev 22:8–9).

"And I fell on my face to worship him; but the angel who was accompanying me would not permit it and said to me, You must not worship any throne or angel that is in the six heavens (that is why I have been sent to accompany you), but you shall worship only him whom I shall tell you to in the seventh heaven" (Ascen. Isa. 7:21–22; trans. R. H. Charles and J. M. T. Barton in Sparks).

Then there is true worship, the worship of the one true God. This explains why there are so many echoes of Deutero-Isaiah (Isa 40–55) in Revelation, for this section of Isaiah places strong emphasis on God's sovereignty over rival gods. For John, true worship is directed toward the one seated on the throne, who alone is worthy "to receive glory and honor and power" (Rev 4:11). Revelation uses the Greek verb *proskynein,* meaning "to prostrate before," "do reverence to," or "worship." This verb can describe showing reverence to angels or humans (it is used this way at 3:9: "Behold I will make them come and fall prostrate at your feet"). But elsewhere in the Apocalypse, it is used in its strong sense of divine worship. That is why worshiping the dragon, the beast, demons, and even an exalted angel are vehemently rejected. Only God is to be worshiped (19:10; 22:9).

Worship is not simply a religious phenomenon. It is also a political and economic issue. The great vision of heavenly worship in Revelation 4 consciously recalls the emperor's throne room in Rome, challenging Rome's claim to universal rule. Several of the seven cities contained temples to the deified emperors, or to the goddess Roma, personification of the city of Rome. Who or what one worships determines one's loyalties and commitments. The cities of Asia had benefitted from Roman rule. Yet Revelation also reveals an underside: Roman domination has come through commercial exploitation and human bloodshed. In the world of the new Babylon, "no one could buy or sell except one who had the stamped image of the beast's name or the number that stood for its name" (13:17). To benefit from Rome's beneficence means being sucked into idolatry, the worship of that which is not God. The Apocalypse unmasks false worship, in all its forms.

WORSHIPING JESUS

Strikingly for a text that is so overtly monotheistic, and rejects even the worship of angels, Revelation incorporates the worship of Jesus into the worship of God. Unlike the angel, who only communicates God's revelation, Christ is the source of that revelation (1:1). Revelation never explicitly uses the verb *proskynein* of Christ, as it does of the one seated on the throne. Still, on several occasions the worship of the Lamb is implied. The Lamb is described as sharing God's throne, the symbol of authentic power, and the focus of divine worship, surrounded by concentric circles of worshipers (the four living creatures, the twenty-four elders, the myriads of angels). Christ has already told the angel of the Laodicean church that he sits with his Father on his throne, having won the victory (3:21). Revelation 5 now describes this enthronement.

The location of the Lamb when John first sees him is ambiguous: "Then I saw standing in the midst of the throne and of the four living creatures and the elders a Lamb that seemed to have been slain" (5:6). This ambiguity is reflected in different English translations of Revelation. It could mean that the Lamb is already sitting on the throne, in the midst of the four living creatures, or that the Lamb is closer to the throne than the four living creatures that surround it (i.e., in between them and the throne). Alternatively, it means that the Lamb is currently standing between the throne, supported by the four living creatures, on the one hand, and the twenty-four elders, on the other. But he is approaching the throne, ready to receive the scroll from the right hand of the one seated on the throne.

TRANSLATIONS OF REVELATION 5:6

Then I saw, in the middle of the throne with its four living creatures and the circle of the elders, a Lamb standing that seemed to have been sacrificed. (NJB)

Then I saw between the throne and the four living creatures and among the elders a Lamb standing as if it had been slaughtered. (NRSV)

> Then I saw a Lamb, looking as if it had been slain,
> standing at the center of the throne, encircled by
> the four living creatures and the elders. (NIV)

> I saw a lamb standing in the center near the throne
> with the four living creatures and the leaders. The
> lamb looked like he had been slaughtered. (God's
> Word Translation)

By the end of this vision, however, the enthronement is complete. A dramatic canticle or doxology, sung by every creature in the universe, ascribes "blessing and honor, glory and might" to the one on the throne *and* to the Lamb (5:13; glory and honor were ascribed to God at 4:11). God and the Lamb are acclaimed together. The response of the elders is to prostrate themselves in worship, as they do elsewhere before God's throne (5:14; cf. 4:10; 11:16; 19:4). The Lamb is now included in this act of divine worship. He continues to share God's throne from this point on (see, e.g., 7:17; 22:1, 3).

Other canticles underscore that the Lamb is to be located on the divine side of the divine/creature divide. There is a striking similarity between the hymns sung in praise of the one seated on the throne (e.g., 4:11; 7:12) and of the Lamb (e.g., 5:12, 13). Both are acclaimed as "worthy…to receive" (4:11; 5:12). If there is a distinction between them, it is in their respective roles in salvation history. The one seated on the throne is worthy because of his role as Creator: "For you created all things; because of your will they came to be and were created" (4:11). The Lamb is worthy in his role as Redeemer: "For you were slain and with your blood you purchased for God those from every tribe and tongue, people and nation" (5:9).

To the one on the throne are ascribed three attributes — "glory and honor and power" (4:11) — three being the number of deity. It parallels his threefold designation as "who was, and who is, and who is to come" (4:8). The Lamb's attributes are sevenfold — "power and riches, wisdom and strength, honor and glory and blessing" (5:12) — a perfect number signifying the totality of the redemption he has won. As God's Messiah, the Lamb is the one by whom God's plan of salvation has been brought to completion.

The canticles or hymns are important because they function as a "running commentary" on the surrounding narrative. They shed important light on the identity and role of the key players, especially the one seated on the throne and the Lamb. But they would also have played an important existential role in sustaining the vision of the small, vulnerable early Christian communities in Asia. As history teaches us, singing has often been central to how protest movements have preserved hope and aspirations for a more just society. We find examples of the power of song elsewhere in the NT. Mary's Magnificat articulates faith in Israel's merciful God who "has thrown down the rulers from their thrones but lifted up the lowly" (Luke 1:52). Paul and Silas sing hymns to God to sustain their hope while in prison in Philippi (Acts 16:25). The hymns of Revelation similarly reassure early Christian audiences that, despite appearance to the contrary, they are on the winning side of a war in which the Lamb has conquered by laying down his life.

CANTICLES IN HONOR OF THE LAMB

Worthy are you to receive the scroll
and to break open its seals,

for you were slain and with your blood you purchased
    for God
those from every tribe and tongue, people and nation.
You made them a kingdom and priests for our God,
and they will reign on earth. (5:9–10)

Worthy is the Lamb that was slain
to receive power and riches, wisdom and strength,
honor and glory and blessing. (5:12)

To the one who sits on the throne and to the Lamb
be blessing and honor, glory and might,
forever and ever. (5:13)

Salvation comes from our God, who is seated on the
    throne,
and from the Lamb. (7:10)

Now have salvation and power come,
and the kingdom of our God
and the authority of his Anointed.
For the accuser of our brothers is cast out,
who accuses them before our God day and night.
They conquered him by the blood of the Lamb
and by the word of their testimony;
love for life did not deter them from death.
Therefore, rejoice, you heavens,
and you who dwell in them.
But woe to you, earth and sea,
for the Devil has come down to you in great fury,
for he knows he has but a short time. (12:10–12)

JESUS AND HIS ANGEL

Another indication that Christ belongs on the divine side of the line separating God from God's creatures is the vision of a mysterious "mighty angel" with a little scroll (10:1–11). This angel descends from heaven, "wrapped in a cloud, with a halo around his head; his face was like the sun and his feet were like pillars of fire" (10:1). As if to demonstrate his exalted status, he stands astride the sea and the land. Ancient audiences might have recalled the Colossus of Rhodes, the 108-foot-high statue of the sun god, Helios, which had once straddled Rhodes Harbor, and whose broken remains could still be seen in John's day. Raising his right hand to heaven, the angel swears by God, "the one who lives forever and ever" (10:6). The resemblance to Daniel's "man clothed in linen" (Dan 10:4–9; 12:6) is strong, for Daniel's angelic figure swears in a similar way:

> The man clothed in linen, who was upstream, lifted his hands to heaven; and I heard him swear by him who lives forever that it should be for a time, two times, and half a time; and that, when the power of the destroyer of the holy people was brought to an end, all these things should end. (Dan 12:7)

John is then invited to take the scroll from the angel's hand, which he eats, finding the words it contains a mixture of sweetness and bitterness (cf. the similar experience of the prophet Ezekiel: Ezek 3:1–4). Early Christians might hear echoes of Jesus's command to "take and eat" (Matt 26:26) in the angel's invitation to "take and swallow it" (Rev 10:9). Like the Eucharist, God's life-giving word is to be devoured. This moment serves as John's recommissioning as a prophet of God: "Then someone said to me, 'You must prophesy again about many peoples, nations, tongues, and kings'" (Rev 10:11).

But who is this angel? The similarities between him and the one like a son of man in 1:12–20 explain why early and medieval Christians thought this was Christ himself. The exalted son of man had feet "like polished brass refined in a furnace," and his face "shone like the sun at its brightest" (1:15–16). The mighty angel's face is also "like the sun" and his feet "like pillars of fire" (10:1). The angel cries out "in a loud voice as a lion roars" (10:3), recalling Christ's title "lion of the tribe of Judah" (5:5; see Gen 49:9). In the prophets, God's speech is sometimes compared to the roaring of a lion (Hos 11:10; Amos 3:8). It would therefore be in character for the divine Christ to roar "as a lion roars."

Yet there are also differences between the two. The angel is clothed in a single cloud, whereas Christ comes "amid the clouds" (Rev 1:7). His fiery feet are similar but not identical to the feet of the son of man. Most strikingly, he swears by "the one who lives forever and ever, who created heaven and earth and sea and all that is in them" (10:6). Though this could refer to the one seated on the throne, the Creator (Rev 4:11; cf. Dan 12:7), Revelation's Christ has already used this phrase of himself: "Once I was dead, but now I am alive forever and ever" (Rev 1:18). This angel therefore swears by the living Christ. He is both like Christ and differentiated from him.

Christ	Mighty Angel
Comes amid the clouds (1:7)	Wrapped in a cloud (10:1)
Feet like polished brass refined in a furnace (1:15)	Feet like pillars of fire (10:1)

Table *continued*

Face like the sun at its brightest (1:16)	Face like the sun (10:1)
Lion of the tribe of Judah (5:5)	Roars like a lion (10:3)
Receives and opens scroll (5:7; 6:1)	Holds an open scroll (10:2)

Most likely the mighty angel is Christ's own angel, first mentioned as the mediator of the "revelation of Jesus Christ" at Revelation 1:1. The idea that nations, and individuals, have their own personal angel is well attested. In Daniel, different nations have their "princes" or angelic patrons (Dan 10:13). Michael is explicitly identified as Israel's protector (12:1). In Matthew's Gospel, Jesus speaks of the "little ones" having their own angels in heaven (Matt 18:10). The Acts of the Apostles contains a story that presupposes that Peter has his own angel (Acts 12:13–15).

But this vision of Jesus's angel describes something more than a guardian angel, underscoring Christ's divine status. John draws upon OT traditions about "the angel of the Lord." This figure was originally a way of speaking about God's visible presence (e.g., Gen 16:10; 22:11; Exod 3:2; Judg 13:3; Zech 3:1–3), though increasingly came to be viewed as a separate, exalted angel functioning as God's mediator (e.g., Matt 1:20; 28:2; Luke 2:9). It is unsurprising that, once Jesus came to be acclaimed as "Lord" (e.g., Acts 2:36; 1 Cor 12:3; Phil 2:11; Jude 14; Rev 11:8; 22:20–21), some early Christians would consider the angel of the Lord to be Jesus's angel. There may be an even more specific reference in Revelation 10. In describing the angel's feet as "like pillars of fire" (10:1), John may be thinking explicitly of the "angel of God" guiding the Israelites through the Red Sea as they embarked on their exodus journey (Exod 14:19). The

Exodus angel manifested himself as "a column," or pillar, "of fiery cloud" (14:24). Revelation's mighty angel therefore provides another reminder that Christ has inaugurated a new Exodus.

CHRIST AND GOD

This chapter has discussed multiple indicators of the close relationship between God and Jesus in the Book of Revelation: Christ the Lamb shares God's throne; Christ is, along with God, the object of worship; hymns sung in praise of Christ echo hymns sung in praise of the deity; Jesus has an angel who resembles the angel of the Lord, or specifically God's angel at the exodus. The discussion in chapter 2 already indicated how titles of God (e.g., "the first and the last," "the Alpha and the Omega," "the beginning and the end," Isa 44:6; Rev 1:8; 21:6) are subsequently transferred to Jesus (Rev 1:17; 22:13). The same may be said of the title "Lord." The Greek word for "Lord" or "master" (*Kurios*) functions as the Greek equivalent for the divine name revealed to Moses, "I am who I am," or YHWH.

In the Apocalypse, "Lord" occurs as a title of the one seated on the throne multiple times. The most frequent usage is in the phrase "the Lord God almighty," occurring the perfect number of seven times (Rev 1:8; 4:8; 11:17; 15:3; 16:7; 19:6; 21:22). This is the Greek equivalent of the Hebrew *YHWH sebaoth* or *YHWH Elohe hasebaoth*, "the Lord (God) of hosts" or "the Lord (God) of armies" (e.g., 2 Sam 5:10; Hos 12:6; Amos 5:15). Variants include "the Lord God" (Rev 18:8; 22:5), "Lord our God" (4:11), "the Lord of the earth" (11:4), "the Lord, the God of prophetic spirits" (22:6), and simply "our Lord" (11:15, mentioned alongside "his Messiah") or "Lord" (15:4).

101

But Revelation also shares the NT conviction that the title "Lord" can also be ascribed to Jesus, by virtue of his resurrection and exaltation to God's right hand (see Acts 2:36; Phil 2:11). Believers now align themselves with his lordship or sphere of influence. His victory over rival claimants to the throne is designated by the title "lord of lords and king of kings (Rev 17:14; cf. 19:6). He is called "their Lord" (i.e., the Lord of the two witnesses, 11:8), who was crucified in the "great city." The book concludes with two prayers for the coming of Jesus as Lord (22:20, 21), recalling the Aramaic prayer known to Paul, *marana tha* (Aramaic for "O Lord, come!," 1 Cor 16:22). Almost certainly, Revelation 14:13 also refers to Jesus: "Blessed are the dead who die in the Lord from now on."

Revelation not only extends divine titles to become titles of Jesus. The close relationship between God and Christ is also found in Christ's actions. As Richard Bauckham has put it, "What Christ does, God does."[2] In the OT, it is God who is Savior of Israel (e.g., Ps 95:1; Isa 45:15; 62:11; Wis 16:7). In Revelation, salvation comes both from God and from the Lamb (7:10; 12:10; 19:1). In Revelation, God fulfills his traditional role as judge (e.g., 6:10; 18:8; cf. Pss 9:9; 96:13; 98:9). But he has also delegated his judgment to Christ, who "judges and wages war in righteousness" (Rev 19:11; cf. Ps 72:2; Isa 11:4–5). In both activities of salvation and judgment, Jesus the Messiah carries out God's work. His coming is God's expected coming as both Judge and Savior. In the Book of Revelation, God is the one "who is and who was and who is to come" (literally "who is coming," 1:4). Seven times throughout the book, Christ also declares "I am coming" or "I am coming quickly" (2:5, 16; 3:11; 16:15; 22:7, 12, 20).

---

2. Bauckham, *Theology*, 63.

Finally, Revelation presents the closeness between Christ and God by using a singular verb or pronoun to denote both together. At the blowing of the seventh trumpet, heavenly voices declare that "the kingdom of the world now belongs to our Lord and to his Anointed, and *he* will reign forever and ever" (11:15). At the end of his description of the New Jerusalem, John writes that "the throne of God and of the Lamb will be in it, and *his* servants will worship him" (22:3). Many manuscripts of 6:17, including Codex Alexandrinus (fifth century CE), have a singular pronoun that elides the one seated on the throne and the wrathful Lamb: "because the great day of *his* wrath has come and who can withstand it?" The practice enables Revelation to identify God and Christ closely, without directly calling Jesus "God" (*theos*). There is a distinction between the one seated on the throne and Jesus, but the two cannot be separated.

SUMMARY

With its dramatic visions of the heavenly liturgy, and memorable canticles in praise of God, Revelation is the NT worship book par excellence. It sharply distinguishes between true worship—the worship of Israel's God, the Creator—and all forms of false worship, whether directed toward the dragon, the beast, demons, or even angels. What is particularly striking is the extent to which the Apocalypse incorporates the worship of Jesus into this true, divine worship. As the slaughtered Lamb, he shares God's throne, to which heavenly worship is directed. Just as hymns are sung in praise of God the Creator, so hymns are sung in praise of Christ as Redeemer. Some hymns are sung in praise of both. Titles of God can be ascribed to Christ. The actions of Christ mirror God's actions.

Early in the second century, Pliny the Younger, governor of Pontus and Bithynia (the Roman province to the north of the province of Asia), wrote to the emperor Trajan that, when Christians gathered together for worship, they would sing a hymn to Christ "as to a god" (*Letters* 10.96). The Apocalypse shows this process already at work in the first century. It seems that the instinct of early Christians to worship Christ precedes the ability to articulate that instinct theologically. The human, crucified Jesus, now risen and glorified, is encountered as divine presence. Hymns may now be sung to the Lamb "as to a god." The Lamb, however, is no second god. He shares in the eternal being of the one, true God.

Conclusion

The Christ of the Apocalypse in the Life of the Church

At the end of this journey through the strange world of the Apocalypse, where do we find ourselves? What has this journey taught us about the Christ we have encountered, and his relationship to his people? This conclusion will reflect on the various images of Christ found in Revelation, and how they function in a complementary way to deepen the church's understanding of Jesus.

The Gospels recount the earthly story of Jesus of Nazareth, particularly his ministry, suffering, death, and resurrection. The Apocalypse of John tells the same story as if from heaven's viewpoint, using vivid apocalyptic symbolism that "makes us see by making things strange." The salvation won through the cross shines forth in the vision of a Lamb standing as if slaughtered (Rev 5:6). The long genealogy tracing Christ's ancestry back to Abraham (Matt 1:2–17) is visualized by the heavenly sign of Israel as a pregnant mother, painfully giving birth to the Messiah (Rev 12:1–6). The expectation of Christ's final coming as judge is presented as the victory procession of the Divine Warrior, accompanied by his martyred cavalry. The crown of thorns, by which the true King is mocked by the agents of Rome, the new Babylon, has been transformed in Revelation's apocalyptic vision into "many diadems" (19:12). The Apocalypse

vividly presents the great gospel irony that Jesus, the crucified victim of the great empire of Rome, is revealed as true
victor, who shares in God's rule over the cosmos, and holds
the angels in the palm of his hand. The medium may be
unfamiliar, but it conveys a familiar message. There is a particularly close affinity with the Gospel of John, for whom
Christ's passion and death is also a glorious victory.

Revelation's vision of the angelomorphic Son of Man (1:9–
20) presents the glorified, divine Christ, whose hair, "white as
white wool or as snow," recalls that of the divine Ancient of
Days seated on the throne (Dan 7:9). His piercing eyes "like
a fiery flame" enable him to see into the human soul, and he
speaks with a resonant divine voice, "like the sound of rushing
water" (see Ezek 43:2). The effect of this vision of the divine
Christ should take the reader's breath away.

Yet this vision also emphasizes Christ's closeness to
his people. As glorified high priest, he stands in the midst
of the seven golden lampstands, that is, in the midst of the
churches. Some scholars hear an echo of that intimate scene
in Eden, where God walked about "in the garden at the
breezy time of the day" (Gen 3:8). Though Christ stands in
judgment over the seven churches (Rev 2 – 3), he also offers
salvation. Even the failing church at Laodicea receives an
invitation: "Behold, I stand at the door and knock. If anyone
hears my voice and opens the door, [then] I will enter his
house and dine with him, and he with me" (3:20). Many
Christians will be familiar with William Holman Hunt's
famous painting of this scene, *The Light of the World*, surviving in three different versions.[1]

Christ as the slaughtered yet standing Lamb is Revelation's christological image par excellence. It vividly
depicts in symbolic form the victory of the cross, bringing

---

1. The three versions are currently displayed in Keble College, Oxford (1849–53),
Manchester City Art Gallery (1851–56), and St. Paul's Cathedral, London (1900–1904).

into dialogue a variety of lamb traditions: a warrior lamb, Isaiah's suffering servant, and especially the Passover lamb. Like other apocalyptic symbols, it stretches the human imagination by juxtaposing images of power and weakness. The Lamb has been slaughtered, yet stands. The Lamb has seven horns (total power) and seven eyes (perfect sight). The lion of the tribe of Judah is Lamb-like in its weakness, yet the sacrifice of the Lamb is a manifestation of leonine power. To quote Brian Blount again, the Lamb "conquers by predatory weakness." That Christ is called "the Lamb" twenty-eight times in the book points to the universal reach of the redemption he brings (seven, symbolizing perfection, multiplied by four, symbolizing the created world). The Lamb's people are the people of the new exodus, freed from sins by the Lamb's blood, and made "into a kingdom, priests for his God and Father" (1:6; cf. Exod 19:6).

Christ as the woman's male child (Rev 12) and the Divine Warrior (19:11–16) reminds readers of the Apocalypse that the victory of Christ involves a real battle. Christ, and his army of martyrs, have confronted evil, oppression, and injustice. But it is essentially a battle won on the cross, signified by the blood on the clothing of the warrior Christ. This is powerfully articulated in the Ascensiontide hymn "See, the Conqueror Mounts in Triumph" by the Victorian Anglican bishop and hymnwriter Christopher Wordsworth.

> Who is this that comes in glory, with the trump of jubilee?
> Lord of battles, God of armies, He has gained the victory.
> He Who on the cross did suffer, He Who from the grave arose,
> He has vanquished sin and Satan, He by death has spoiled His foes.

CHRIST IN THE BOOK OF REVELATION

(Christopher Wordsworth, 1862; in the public domain)

As the Divine Warrior, Christ also comes as judge, speaking the sword-like word of truth, and unmasking deception and falsehood. He does so "in righteousness" or "in justice" (19:11), as Israel's king was meant to do. Revelation's first audiences would have heard this vision as a powerful indictment of Rome's dark side. But the image has perennial significance. An English medieval legend recounts how St. Hugh of Lincoln, the twelfth-century Carthusian bishop, pointed to a sculpture of Christ the apocalyptic judge, to warn England's King John of the consequences of an unjust rule.

The Christology of the Apocalypse is also closely connected to the theme of worship. The worship of Jesus is incorporated into the worship of the one true God, who sits on the divine throne. The book offers a recurring vision of the heavenly liturgy, in which angels minister as priests. The earliest Christian communities in Asia likely heard this book in a liturgical context, perhaps when gathered for the Eucharist. Given the prominence the Apocalypse gives to worship, many Catholics will be puzzled as to why it appears so rarely in the church's liturgy. As noted in the introduction, only a small number of passages occur in the Roman Sunday lectionary (excerpts from chaps. 1, 5, 7, 21, and 22). The book is also read at Mass on the Solemnities of the Assumption (11:19a; 12:1–6a, 10ab) and All Saints (7:2–4, 9–14), and at the Chrism Mass on Holy Thursday (1:5–8). In total, this comprises only 51 of the book's 406 verses. The daily Mass lectionary provides a more extensive coverage, although even here major sections of Revelation are absent. In addition, excerpted canticles from Revelation are said or sung several days a week at Evening Prayer. Only those who pray the Office of Readings will read the Apocalypse in its entirety.

CANTICLES FROM REVELATION IN THE DIVINE OFFICE

Rev 4:11; 5:9–10, 12 (Hymn of the redeemed)
Rev 11:17–18; 12:10b–12a (The judgment of God)
Rev 15:3–4 (Hymn of adoration)
Rev 19:1–2, 5–7 (The marriage feast of the Lamb)

Despite the paucity of readings from Revelation in the Sunday lectionary, there is significance in the fact that several of these appear in the Easter season of Year C. There is an "Easter hermeneutic" at work here that is very ancient. The practice of reading Revelation after Easter is attested in the churches of Gaul, Spain, and Portugal. In Rome, it was read in the Octave of Pentecost.[2] The preservation of this ancient custom in the modern church means that Revelation is read through the lens of Christ's victory, as the Paschal Lamb who overcame death and inaugurated the new exodus. It explains the apocalyptic symbolism of many Easter hymns: "At the Lamb's high feast we sing praise to our victorious king." "From death to life eternal, from earth unto the sky, our Christ hath brought us over, with hymns of victory." The Christ of the Apocalypse brings his people from slavery to freedom, from death to life. The church celebrates, and lives out, that victory in liturgy, in song, in visual art. Christ has died. Christ is risen. Christ will come again.

---

2. For a discussion of the liturgical use of Revelation across the centuries, see Ian Boxall, "The Book of Revelation in the Life of the Church," *Josephinum Journal of Theology* 23, nos. 1–2 (2016): 160–75.

Select Bibliography

Bauckham, Richard. *The Theology of the Book of Revelation.* Cambridge: Cambridge University Press, 1993.

Blount, Brian K. *Can I Get a Witness? Reading Revelation through African American Culture.* Louisville, KY: Westminster John Knox Press, 2005.

Boxall, Ian. *The Revelation of Saint John.* Black's NT Commentaries. Peabody, MA: Hendrickson, 2006.

Collins, Adela Yarbro. *Crisis and Catharsis: The Power of the Apocalypse.* Philadelphia: Westminster Press, 1984.

Kiel, Micah D. *Apocalyptic Ecology: The Book of Revelation, the Earth, and the Future.* Collegeville, MN: Liturgical Press, 2017.

Koester, Craig R. *Revelation: A New Translation with Introduction and Commentary.* AYB 38A. New Haven, CT: Yale University Press, 2014.

Kovacs, Judith, and Christopher Rowland. *Revelation: The Apocalypse of Jesus Christ.* Blackwell Bible Commentaries. Malden, MA: Blackwell, 2004.

Moloney, Francis J. *The Apocalypse of John: A Commentary.* Grand Rapids: Baker Academic, 2020.

Nusca, A. Robert. *The Christ of the Apocalypse: Contemplating the Faces of Jesus in the Book of Revelation.* Steubenville, OH: Emmaus Road Publishing, 2018.

O'Hear, Natasha, and Anthony O'Hear. *Picturing the Apocalypse: The Book of Revelation in the Arts over Two Millennia.* Oxford: Oxford University Press, 2015.

Rhoads, David, ed. *Every People and Nation: The Book of Revelation in Intercultural Perspective*. Minneapolis: Fortress, 2005.

Rowland, Christopher. "The Book of Revelation." In *The New Interpreter's Bible*, ed. L. E. Keck, 12:503–743. Nashville: Abingdon Press, 1998.

Schüssler Fiorenza, Elisabeth. *The Book of Revelation: Justice and Judgment*. Philadelphia: Fortress, 1985.